PETEE - THE ISLANDER

PETEE

STEVEN J. ZEVITAS

IUNIVERSE, INC.
BLOOMINGTON

PETEE - THE ISLANDER
PETEE

iUniverse books may be ordered through booksellers or by contacting:

*iUniverse
1663 Liberty Drive
Bloomington, IN 47403
www.iuniverse.com
1-800-Authors (1-800-288-4677)*

*Because of the dynamic nature of the Internet, any Web addresses or links contained in this book
may have changed since publication and may no longer be valid.*

*ISBN: 978-1-4502-7322-0 (sc)
ISBN: 978-1-4502-7323-7 (dj)
ISBN: 978-1-4502-7324-4 (ebk)*

Printed in the United States of America

iUniverse rev. date: 1/11/2011

DEDICATION

TO THE STUDENTS, INSTRUCTORS AND STAFF WHO HAVE HONORED THE BOYS SCHOOL ON THOMPSON'S ISLAND, BOSTON, MASSACHUSETTS

BOSTON ASYLUM AND FARM SCHOOL FOR INDIGENT BOYS

(circa 18th century)

THE FARM AND TRADE SCHOOL

(circa 20th century)

THOMPSON ACADEMY (circa 20th century)

ACCOMPLISHMENTS

Designed educationally - "Learn-by-doing."

First school boy band in America.

Introduced animal husbandry.

Introduced first "Self Government" program.

Developed Swedish "Sloyd" woodworking.

Intra-mural sports program.

State-wide sports program.

Dear Father.
We thank thee for life and health,
For friends and all we have
Help us to play the man

Beautiful Isle of Thompson
Set in a sea of blue,
Molding our hearts together,
Making us into men true.

Working - Playing,
Life is just what you make it boys,
Friends of good cheer you'll find them here,
Beautiful Isle of Thompson.

CONTENTS

No matter when - no matter where - no matter how there are stories in every period of a boy's existence when a teenager finds he must hurdle the stumbling blocks of life to survive. His decisions can grip his weakness or it can simply challenge him. This is a story of a teenager struggling with his identity, forcing him to seize life's fragile formula and shake it to make sense of its wisdom. This is the tale of -

PETEE

CHAPTER ONE

JUNE 1941

Thompson's Island was bequeathed by Miles Standish to his English friend David Thompson who came to America and took up residence on the island. We move ahead from those early Settler days to where local businessmen of Boston took pity on the wayward youth roaming the streets during the eighteen hundreds and established a facility next door to Paul Revere's house. This popular solution was soon flooded by these wandering youth.

The businessmen then purchased the vacated Thompson's Island where a farm and trade school was established. This type of program was fully operational for over one hundred years. In recognition of the wisdom and dedication by the sponsors of this unique school thousands of graduates went on to live productive lives. The novel "PETEE" follows one boy's journey into a restructured life.

A twelve year old stood on a dock awaiting a tugboat to take him across the bay to an island boy's school, in 1941. The youngster had met the strict criteria for acceptance where the rules stipulated he had to come from a broken home and above all, not be able to afford the tuition.

From his early beginnings the boy's mother was shut up in a mental institution where nine years later she died, for the mental institution also harbored a tuberculosis sanatorium and from there the dreaded disease took her life. His father struggled to care for six children after losing his business to the economic crisis of 1929.

A catastrophic fire destroyed what was left in memories of a crumbling middle class life. Now, forced to accept a wretched life that spiraled into the poverty of a cold water, unheated tenement. The struggle to survive continued despite rumblings of war in Europe.

Young Peter Pappas accepted being separated from his twin sister and four brothers - brothers who were soon to be drafted for war. He now faced a different type of challenge in his young life for the twelve year old had to shift for himself. On the distant island he would meet a family of boys who also came from broken homes, each of whom had to struggle through a new learning experience.

Some seven years have passed where we meet a seventeen year old Peter Pappas atop a bluff overlooking the sea at the south end of the island. It was a June day in nineteen forty-eight, just a few years after a war where a dazzling display of fighting ships filled the distant natural harbor. Peter, a lithe, athletically built youth regretted that he was not able to join the army as had his four older brothers. He was only fifteen when the war ended in nineteen forty-five, still too young to close the war.

Now dangling his legs over the bluff he braced himself while looking into the cloudless sky where stark white Sea Terns soared nimbly along hidden air currents. Cutting, shrieking cries made one think that panic had seized the birds. A little over a mile away the city of Boston looked shrouded in a haze, enveloped like a fuzzy cocoon. He took a deep breath, filling his lungs with the fresh salty smell of the sea. The air smelled so pure.

He draped his arms over his knees and gripped his shins with his hands, then rested his chin on knobby knees. A gentle breeze ruffled a cow-lick dangling over his forehead, it was a perpetual problem he had to live with all these years, but it didn't matter. He focused on a small yacht slicing through the water, it's bow raised to the foamy sea in a miniature tempest. Suddenly, a deep scowl crossed the boy's brow. His eyes narrowed into thin slits when he pictured his return home, now scheduled later in that afternoons graduation. His lips curled in loathing when he pictured himself going back to the teeming streets of the tenement he had left so many years ago.

His memories flashed gently at first, rose in a whirlwind then immediately subsided into more gentle thoughts. He smiled to himself when he remembered an Autumn day in nineteen forty-one when his oldest brother Lou drove him to the pier at City Point. It was a public landing which was crowded with other boys who looked about his own age. They too looked troubled just as Peter was. Suitcases lined the pier, some bags strapped together with belts while others bared split corners disclosing untold years of wear.

Peter was afraid of what lay ahead. He had never dreamed he would ever live at a boarding school, much less be separated from his twin sister Anna all at one time. His thoughts flashed to Anna, an incurable, tenderhearted girl who's tears rendered him so helpless when they said goodbye. But, this was not the time to show even a hint of misgiving in front of Lou. All of his brothers teased him about his own sensitive nature, something he knew he inherited from an obscure memory he held of his mother.

A small tug boat approached the pier. The young boy had read school literature that the Pilgrim III would ferry the new students to the island. A teenage crew dressed in flared sailor pants with snug navy blue pullover jersey's looked the very part of sailors Peter had seen in magazines. The pullovers were topped with stark white sailor caps set jauntily on their heads. As if on cue the boat boys hustled to make the craft secure to a float.

Peter was full of envy when he saw the ponderous tug anchored so precisely by the boys a bit older than himself. "I'm gonna do that, some day." he thought to himself. Suddenly, his brother's voice interrupted his fantasy. He turned to face Lou who spoke softly, "Petee, I'm gonna have to leave you kid. I've got to get to work."

The twelve year old stoically met his brother's guilty look. The boy listened as his brother continued, "You can make it on your own, kid." He smiled at his little brother when he wrapped the boy into his arms and hugged him.

Peter shoved his hands into his pant pockets, turned from his brother and looked off into the harbor. His eyes were fixed on the distant Thompson's Island where he would be sleeping that night. "Yea." He answered, his voice a thread above a whisper. He gulped with difficulty for he felt an urge to cry, and yet, he struggled with all of his might to fight the tears away.

"It's okay, Lou." He answered without turning. Lou squeezed the boy's shoulder and whispered in his ear, "Go out there Petee, and be a king."

When he turned to face his brother, Lou had disappeared. The boy stared longingly at the parking lot when he heard the engine of the old Desoto rumble loudly, gears meshed noisily and then the car was gone. An isolated tear slipped down his cheek which he quickly rubbed with the back of his hand. He bit his lower lip and turned to face the Pilgrim III which was rocking gently at the dock. He looked down the pilings which held up the dock where years of crusted ooze had turned a vulgar, slimy green color. The incoming tide pushed frothy waves that spit like a hissing cat when it receded. Peter wrinkled his nose at the smelly waterlogged pilings.

"Some day," he promised himself, "I won't need any of 'em." A smile twitched his lips when he continued, "Well, maybe I'll need Dad and Anna and Chris and Nick and John and Tony," he thought for a moment and added, "even Lou." His smile faded after he named every one of those left in his family. His eyes fell on a man standing on the bow of the boat. The boy pursed his lips and frowned down on the pier and said with finality, "But, I won't need nobody else."

A voice suddenly called from the boat: "All students going to the Farm and Trade School board the boat now, please." The man on the bow of the boat was having a problem with wire framed eye glasses that slipped to his flared nostrils. "Okay boys!" he called again when he pulled the glasses off his face and used them as a pointer.

"Everyone on board, please. Say your goodbye's" He no sooner spoke when two sharp blasts from the ship's horn startled everyone. Looks of astonishment filled the faces of parents and friends who were saying their goodbye's.

Peter struggled with his suitcase and scampered down the gangway. He felt more nervous now that he got closer to the boat for this was going to be his first ever boat ride. Finally, he reached the docked boat that suddenly looked so huge now that he was standing next to it. He turned to see if the others had followed him, he was alone. Hunching his shoulders he turned his back on the lot of them, then swung his suitcase so it barely cleared the boat's railing where it slammed noisily next to the cabin door. The momentum of the awkward toss made him lose his balance forcing him to grab hold of the boat's bumper which was sandwiched against the float to prevent damage to the hull.

Clinging to the bumper he suddenly panicked when he unknowingly put pressure against the boat forcing the steamer to slowly drift away from the float. Horror was etched on his face when he found himself spread-eagle, his feet on the float while his hands clutched the bumper of the drifting boat. Peter's heart thundered in his chest for he was sure he was about to plunge into the murky water; he could not swim.

Suddenly, the lines secured to the cleats prevented the Pilgrim III from drifting further, the large boat slowly returned toward the float. The young offender felt a rush of relief when his footing became more solid on the float. He looked up to see a boat boy glaring down at him, the young sailor's eyes were fixed in stony disapproval.

"Hey! You! New Johnnie! That's no way to treat this boat!" the young islander snapped when he gripped Peter's wrist, then hauled him forcefully aboard. "You don't throw your bag on the deck like that." He continued to admonish the frightened youth, "It'll scratch the paint on the bulkhead, you jerk!" It did not matter that the twelve year old had a terrible experience. The older boy simply kicked the upturned suitcase and snapped, "Get this thing aft and wait for the others."

Peter stared in surprise. His shoulder ached after being hauled on board with such force. The boat boy had disappeared when the youngster gripped his bag and struggled to the rear deck which he presumed was 'aft' and what was this 'bulkhead' thing? The strange terms simply confused him. Finally, he stood as far to the rear of the boat as he could get and watched the other boys also crowd the stern with their luggage.

He was rubbing his aching shoulder when suddenly a curly haired man stood in front of him He recognized him as the man who had been standing on the front of the boat.

"What's your name, son?" he asked.

Peter looked into the man's inquiring blue eyes masked behind wire framed glasses. "They call me Petee." His lips tightened into a nervous grin.

The man's eyes focused on the boy unflinchingly when he corrected, "They call me Petee, SIR!" The accented 'SIR!" stunned the boy. He looked confused when the youngster asked, "What?"

"Whenever you speak to an adult at our school you will always say, SIR or MA-Am!" His emphasis lay heavily on the words 'SIR and 'MA-AM!

It was Peter's first lesson. It made him uncomfortable, especially with attention of the other new boys fixed on him. The twelve year old took a step back when he came in contacts with a metal railing. "Yes, S-S-Sir." he answered meekly when the blood drained his face. An amused smile flashed at the youth by the stern adult. He then said, "I'm Mister Clifton, son." The muscles in Clifton's face relaxed. His eyes softened as they circled the youthful face. "That's the kind of student we like here. One who learns fast." Yellow, tobacco stained teeth smiled fondly at the rigid boy. "Don't you agree, Peter?" he asked.

Peter gulped at Clifton's question, "Sir?" he spoke hesitatingly and finally answered a bit more aggressively, "My name's Petee." He sucked his breath. Saucer eyes stared up at the adult whose smile slowly waned.

Clifton's brow knit into a frown. A series of ridges forced his eyebrows to form a peculiar pinched expression around his eyes. "Petee what?" he asked obviously annoyed.

The boy's voice was stronger when he responded quickly, "Petee Pappas, Sir." He gave a nervous smile for he did not know what to expect from the stranger.

The Instructor scanned his roster and then looked at the boy over the tops of his glasses. Searching eyes were fixed on the youngster. "On this roster it lists you as Peter Pappas, young man." He waited for an explanation. The twelve year old gulped when he took a quick look at the inquiring faces of the other new boys. He then fixed his eyes on Clifton's scuffed shoes and mumbled, "Everyone calls me, Petee." His temples pulsed with the beat of his heart. "Sir!" Clifton corrected.

Peter's eyes glistened with suppressed tears. He turned his face and focused his eyes on the swelling ocean. Suddenly, raindrop size droplets cascaded down his cheeks. "S-S-Sir!" He struggled with his use of the strange word, then abruptly turned his back on the adult for he was humiliated that he cried in front of the other new boys.

Clifton eyed him critically, then a grin appeared on his face, "I think you and I will get along just fine, Peter." In one motion of dismissal he turned to greet the other new boys who had watched in fascination at the showdown between student and adult.

Suddenly, the engine roared to life. The deck vibrated when the propeller churned the water convulsively. Bubbles hissed with the revolving thrust of the twisted blades. Peter stared dumbfounded when the sea churned, eddying into whirlpools of bubbling agitation. The large craft slowly backed away from the landing. It was then the twelve year old realized his feet were tingling from the vibrations.

Peter relaxed and drew a deep breath of air, now finding it an odd mixture with the smells from the sea and those of the boat's gas and oil emissions. He gripped the vibrating metal railing and smiled at himself when his fingers pulsed in a rhythm with the engine. For the moment he forgot his encounter with Mister Clifton. The Pilgrim Ill's engine slipped into a hasty rumble when the boy looked back at the diminishing pier. Suddenly, Boston's tall buildings erupted in his view like towering mountains. The sun glistened on windows that seemed to dance like flitting fairies on beds of fleecy clouds.

Peter had never been taken to downtown Boston and now questions raged in his mind about what it would be like to walk those strange streets. He searched his mind to find if there was ever one time he might have been taken from the tenement and the streets of Roxbury to what he remembered his brothers saying was 'down town", but, there was no memory of that.

His whole world was made up of those Roxbury streets. Running to the store for his Dad meant crossing the old cobblestone Ruggles Street at the end of the tenement. He knew every inch of the alleys between neighboring equally similar tenements that made up his neighborhood. He knew the stray cats and where they had their litters. It was easy for the momma cat to feed herself when she had her litter near the garbage cans. From Peter's bed he heard the cat fights and oh, how he wished he were outside to throw rocks at them. But Yia Yia, his grandmother, would not tolerate his behavior.

When Yia Yia died his whole world collapsed, for she meant so much to him. His underwear went unchanged and his feet smelled. Yia Yia bathed him in the kitchen sink. He dreaded having his hair washed because it meant fear of covering his eyes with a cloth towel; he was so afraid of the dark. Anna and he took turns at the sink because they had no bathtub, no shower, just a simple toilet. The brothers showered at a local bath house.

And now Yia Yia was gone and there was no time for baths. Dad worked long hours, struggling to keep the family together. Peter understood what Dad was going through despite the youngster's age -what was it now, eight or nine or so. It was the smell of Dad's cigar that gave Peter a feeling of security. Dad left for work at six in the morning, leaving a lingering, pungent, cigar smell which gave Peter comfort and safekeeping to the troubled youth. Flies filled every room, where they found their way through unscreened windows only to find their doom on sticky paper hanging from the single suspended light bulb in the kitchen. Peter often wondered if flies lived on islands.

When Mom died Yia Yia fell apart having lost her only daughter "In that place". One day, Peter and Anna, rummaged through an old chest where they discovered long brown hair laying neatly across the tops of clothing. The twins, conspiratorially, settled on the premise that Yia Yia had secretly placed those hairs in the chest.. On more than one occasion they removed the silky strands and gently stroked them. Anna, who also was absorbed with this mystery would patiently untangle the strands that had become entwined.

Yia Yia, aware that the children were too quiet, caught them. They expected a spanking, but all she did was to gather up the tresses and almost reverently replace them in the chest. A sympathetic look from Yia Yia ended the escapade, for it seemed the mystery had been solved by all of them, no explanation was necessary. Now distracted from their curious inspection, the two miscreants slipped away to play.

Whenever Peter asked Yia Yia about the hair she tossed him a vague explanation, certainly not enough for an inquisitive boy. "It's Mamma's hair, huh, Yia Yia?" he blurted it out one day. The Grandmother's shoulders stiffened. She glanced at the inquisitive blue eyes staring at her, then immediately turned back to the dishes she was washing in the sink. Raising her arm she wiped an eye and then noisily clattered the dishes. "You cut her hair before they took her to that place. Huh, Yia Yia."

8

"ENOUGH!" she snapped. For the first time Peter saw her eyes glisten with tears. Her lower lip trembled only to be covered with wrinkled fingers. Peter slowly back away. He eyed the door in case he had to flee, but he gave up the thought and reached out to Yia Yia. She wrapped him against her bosom and gently pushed her fingers through his hair. Neither of them spoke for they both wept softly. Finally, she held him at arms length and said, "Peter, first comes God. He has all the answers."

Peter gazed into the harbor where he saw other boats anchored off shore. Soon they passed them and here the ocean turned a deep green, except where the Pilgrim pushed the white foamy waters aside. He was suddenly aware that chatter had stopped between the other new boys, for they were looking toward the front of the boat, their eyes fixed on an island looming directly ahead.

The twelve year old glanced far to his right and then quickly to his left, forever capturing the rhythm of the waves charging the shore like silver sparklers that he lit on Fourth of July. The Pilgrim slowed its forward thrust, then drifted toward a float where it was to be tied up.

The youngster was dazzled by the massive pilings holding up the towering wharf, they too were filled with the same crusted green ooze he saw at City Point. A simple smile appeared on the boy's face for the pilings became a vision of hundreds of soldiers standing at attention. And then, he saw them as tall, elegant trees in a forest, where row upon row of the giants blocked his view.

There was only one time he saw a forest - a real forest. Yia Yia, Anna and his brother Nick spent a summer on a farm. There, surrounding the whole place were trees, thick trees, skinny trees, trees bent in odd shapes and others split in half. Anna and he must have been six or seven. When they arrived Ma-Ma was there waiting for them. Could this be "that place" mentioned by Yia Yia? Peter thought. An anxious fear gripped him, but he kept it to himself.

Peter stood to one side when Yia Yia enveloped her daughter in a tearful embrace. The boy gulped nervously. His eyes were fastened on the woman with the stark sallow face. For an instant he pictured long brown hair draped over her shoulders only to see scissors hack them away. A chill rushed through him when he took a step closer. Dark brown eyes sparkling with tears were fastened on the confused boy.

She dropped to one knee and wrapped Anna in her large arms. Kisses smothered the little girl. Stubby fingers traced through the young girl's hair. Peter wiped his hand across his lips when he took another hesitating step closer. He waited to be hugged by this woman he had only heard of in whispers. Wide eyed and confused, Peter gulped nervously. Suddenly, Ma Ma reached for him and hauled him into her arms where his unyielding body seemed like it was rooted in the soil. He felt like gagging when her tears moistened his face. Wet lips spread distasteful salty kisses across his mouth. With Anna locked in one arm and Peter surrounded by the other the two were pressed into her breasts. Finally, with his head next to her ear, the boy managed to wipe his face on the simple cotton print dress that loosely fit her shoulder.

From up on the wharf a whistle blew. All heads turned as one when a band filled the air with a vibrant medley of marches. Groups of schoolboys gathered at the railing where their voices carried over the blare of the band and down to those on the float below. "Hey you guys," one voice yelled, "Welcome to Thompson's." Another student shouted, "Yea, lots-a-luck you guys." It was followed by laughter. A shrill whistle cut above the band's music, but that did not hold back happy voices shouting down to the new boys.

Peter pulled on his suitcase when the boat docked and then scrambled onto the float which led to a steep gangway rising up to the wharf. At the top of the gangway a large mass of students jostled each other while they waited impatiently for the new boys to come up and on to the wharf. Clifton called a roll call of the New Johnnies then smiled with a remark, "I guess we didn't lose anybody overboard." He looked at Peter and winked when the other boys chuckled nervously at his joke.

It was a tortuous climb for the twelve year old for the gangway had pitched steeply due to the low tide. Now breathless, he finally reached the top. Suddenly, a hand grabbed his suitcase and pulled it away from him. Peter, taken by surprise lunged for the satchel only to be blocked by two other boys. The youngster's adrenalin surged when he thought he had to fight on his first day.

"It's okay, Johnnie." The boy with his suitcase spoke from the edge of the crowd. He flashed a broad smile at the confused student. "I'm gonna carry it for you, pal."

Two older boys sandwiched Peter between them while the third carried his bag. "What's your name, Johnnie?" The boy asking the question placed his arm across Peter's shoulders. At the far end of the wharf the band was parading toward the graded walk which passed an enormous white barn. Music vibrated through the trees while the new student watched the uniformed band members keenly. "I'm gonna do that." The thought dangled enviously in his mind.

"Hey, Johnnie. I asked you a question." The student squeezed Peter's shoulders firmly, giving him a friendly shake. The twelve year old looked confused when he glanced back to see if his bag was still close to him. "My....MY name's Petee. Sir." He finally answered.

"Hey, you don't call us Sir." The others chuckled at his naivete'. "Only teachers and instructors are called Sir." Another boy continued, "Your name's not Petee. For the first year at the school your name's, JOHNNIE!" he emphasized the name for effect.

"What did you say?" Peter asked incredulously.

"Yea, all the new kids are called, NEW JOHNNIE'S. That's so we know everyone of you guys by name." He gave Peter a gentle nudge with his hip, "Don't-cha-get-it?" he teased.

They reached the base of a wide stone covered walk. The band had neared the top of a hill that rose toward a ponderous red bricked building. The new student was overwhelmed with his reception and discovered the tension was slowly leaving him, he was calming down. With wide-eyed curiosity he stared at the massive wall of the white barn they were passing. "What's in there? He asked innocently. The boy struggling with Peter's suitcase answered, "Cows." Another boy said, "Horses." The third boy continued, "Goats and bulls and hay and straw and even a pasteurizing room."

Peter looked in awe when they passed the barn. He then said, "I was on a farm once, but they didn't have any cows or horses or anything else." He squirreled his nose disdainfully, "Just lousy chickens."

"Over there." The student closest to Peter pointed to a cluster of small white buildings. "A thousand Rhode Island Reds in there. And way out there," he continued to point at the south end of the island, "that's the farm where we grow corn and beans, beets, potatoes, squash and turnips and...."

"What's Rhode Island Reds?" Peter interrupted.

The boys laughed at his innocence when someone answered, "They're chickens."

It took but a moment when Peter recaptured that day on the farm with Yia Yia and Ma Ma. The farmer took Peter by the hand and hauled him toward a wire fence where the chickens were wandering aimlessly outside the enclosure. Anger was riveted on the old farmer's face. He was mumbling to himself about having his head examined for letting this family stay on his farm.

Finally, the gruff old man stopped where a portion of the fence had been ripped out of the ground leaving a gaping hole large enough for a person to slip through. The wizened old farmer glared down at the boy who's eyes were fixed on the damage. "Ya done this, didn't-cha-boy?" his raspy surly voice snapped. Peter's jaw dropped open when the farmer yanked his wrist and snarled again, "Ya done this, didn't-cha, boy!" Hollow blue eyes looked up at the rugged, furious man. Peter gulped for he knew instantly that Ma Ma probably did it. He stared numbly at the damage.

"The chickens, boy! They coulda run away. Now I gotta fix this mess." Yellowed teeth flashed behind his sneer. He squeezed Peter's wrist until it hurt. "Did ya do this, boy?"

Peter tried to pull his wrist out of the old man's grip, but it was useless to even try. He shifted his feet and looked down, then answered softly, "Yea, I did it."

"WHY!" the anguished voice of the old man filled the yard. Pain was etched in the farmer's eyes. His hand trembled when he pointed at the gaping hole, "I gotta do other things 'round her, boy. You've made more work for me." He spun the petrified youth around and kicked his fanny while releasing him. Peter fled toward the house. "Do that agin, boy and I'll womp the tar out of ya, then I'll kick the bunch of ya off this farm." The angry voice drifted with the wind.

Peter raced away where he found Anna. The children huddled together at the corner of the farm house. The boy looked down pensively when he related the story to his horrified sister. Anna looked teary-eyed at her brother when a secret agreement of covering-up passed between the seven year olds. There was nothing else to be said.

It was the next day, a Sunday, when the family expected Dad's weekly visit. Peter usually waited by the farm house with Anna, watching the dirt road for the familiar figure that seemed to appear from the woods like a giant. Suspended from strings his fingers dangled a square white box which the children recognized as a pie from the bakery where Daddy worked.

A straw hat, laced by a brilliantly colored ribbon at the brim set jauntily on top of the rugged man's head. All of this accented the strong, rigid lines on his squared handsome face. Since it was Sunday he religiously wore a suit despite the heat of the summer's day. His necktie was securely fixed to the collar of his shirt. And there, hanging from his lips the curved pipe was a fixture where dusky gray puffs of smoke signaled its bowl was crammed with enough tobacco to last the long walk from the bus stop to the farm.

But, this Sunday Peter did not wait for his twin sister Anna to join him. He raced along the dirt road and fled past huge overhanging trees that lined each side of the compacted earthen course. Suddenly, he stopped abruptly. Swirls of dust fell like a cloud around his sneakers. A tangle of hair formed a cowlick on a furrowed, perplexed brow. Deep blue eyes were stonily fixed on a bushy tailed skunk that dominated the road ahead. Glossy black accented a white stripe on it's back that raced all the way up its perpendicular tail. Peter's heart raced rapidly when the skunk's eyes linked with those of the terrified boy.

He knew better than to challenge the animal for he knew he could be the recipient of its foul smell. The skunk took two more steps and stopped again to cast a wary eye at the motionless intruder. The animal then let out a sharp cry, signaling at a movement from the weedy growth where four miniature skunks scurried clumsily after their mother.

The boy's frozen eyes softened. A quick smile filled his face. "They're so cute." he spoke aloud. A tempting urge to cuddle the adorable infants raced through his mind, but once again caution prevailed. And then they were gone. Peter picked his way along the road. His eyes were fixed where the threatening menace had disappeared. For the first time he breathed a sigh of relief when he put some distance between himself and the skunk.

He arrived breathlessly to a few yards from the highway and sat on a large rock where his knees became a resting place for the seven year olds chin. His fingers aimlessly formed circles and squares in the dirt while he waited anxiously. Solemn eyes searched the length of the empty road only to return disappointedly to the scored lines he was scratching into the earth.

He grit his teeth when he whispered aloud, "That meany farmer's not gonna blame me again. If he hits Anna, I'm gonna.... I'm gonna...." His small fist swung in the air, "I'm gonna sock him, that's what I'm gonna do." Suddenly, he saw the straw hat just above thick bushes which hugged a corner of the road. The boy leaped to this feet and raced to his father who had barely time to remove his pipe and set the squared white box on the ground to embrace his charging son. The boy plunged into his outstretched arms while teary eyed words tumbled from his mouth. "The fence was pulled up and the chickens got away and Daddy, the farmer blamed me and he got real mad and then I found a broken window and Mamma locked us all out of the house, and....and....I'm gonna get blamed again." His sobs were suddenly muffled when his father pressed the boy into his chest.

The father's face turned ashen when he finally grasped the child by his shoulders and slowly wiped the youths tears with his handkerchief. The only sounds were of Peter sniffing away his tears. "Daddy," he asked, "Is Mamma....? Is Mamma....?" Gulping deeply he felt the rush of frustration for he feared he was asking a grown-up question - a question that little boys do not ask. His hand was held by his father when they started down the dirt road and it was here he knew from past experiences when his father did not speak a little boy kept his distance. But, the boy's question had to be answered. He was seven years old now and not that little kid of a few years ago.

Finally, he blurted, "Yia Yia always tells us Mamma is in "that place", Daddy. He looked up at this father's grim face, but the boy persisted. "Anna and me found all this brown hair in a chest and when we asked Yia Yia who's it was she chased us away." He felt his hand being squeezed, yet there still was no answer from his father. "Now Momma's here, Daddy. Is this "that place" Yia Yia keeps telling us? "And," he gulped nervously, "this stuff that's happening....I tell the farmer I did it cuz....cuz...." his voice trailed off.

Tears slipped down his cheeks when suddenly his father stopped walking to relight his pipe, but as hard as he tried he could not get it lit. Peter was sure he was in for a beating even though his father never, ever, beat him. The squared box had been set on the ground and now for sure the boy thought the spanking was about to happen. Suddenly, his father knelt on the ground and embraced his son, he then asked, "Petee, do you know where your mother lives?

The boy's eyes faltered when he answered softly, "I think she's in a hospital, Daddy."

"And do you know why she's in a hospital?" he asked.

Peter drew a deep breath and answered with his own question, "It's cuz she's sick, ain't it, Daddy?"

There was a momentary pause when the adult asked, "What kind of sickness do you think she has, my boy?" The pipe was tapped on a small rock with the burned contents spilling onto the ground. Peter nervously sucked in his breath again for his deepest suspicions were about to be discussed. He finally answered, "Anna and me think she's....," his voice drifted into a frightened whisper, "We....We think....she's crazy, Daddy." He quickly pulled away from his father, stepping back a few paces and waited in fear that certainly now he would get the beating of his life.

His father continued to kneel in the middle of the road. His head was bowed and ever so slowly he removed his straw hat baring silver strands of thinning hair. Finally, he set his hat back on his head and took a deep breath, exhaling slowly when he raised his eyes so they focused on the distraught child. Finally, he spoke softly, "No, Petee. Mamma is not crazy." He spoke calmly, reassuringly. The youth's gripping stare locked on his father when the adult continued, "Mamma is the hospital because she's very sick. But, soon she's going to get well and she'll come home to take care of all of us." He smiled closed-lipped when he beckoned the boy to come to him.

Confident now that he would not get a beating for what he had said, he slipped his hand into his father's free hand and the two strode on toward the farm house. The adult finally said, "Don't worry about the farmer, Petee. I'll speak to him so he doesn't blame you anymore."

Peter looked up into his father's smiling face and said, "Oh Daddy, I'm glad you're here."

In moments they were overwhelmed by the sudden arrival of a breathless Anna. She was swept into the arms of her father and twirled in a giggling embrace. As she was swirled around the twins locked eyes on each other where a recognition in their bond to one another put to rest the girl's silent question - for all was well.

Peter and his new friends finally arrived at the top of the hill where a massive red bricked building dominated the highest point on the island. Four Ionic columns stood out starkly, standing like sentinels guarding the entry. Peter arched his neck back, now looking straight up at the huge building. His lips moved imperceptibly for the building reminded him of the fire when he was six years old.

It was just a flash of memory when he was interrupted when one of the students said, "It's called Bulfinch. It's where we go to class. You know....where everything happens." He pointed to a small balcony tucked behind the Ionic columns, "Headmaster's office is right up there. We call him Moley cuz he's got a big mole right here." he pointed to his own chin, "like right here."

From the side of the building Clifton's voice could be heard calling the new boys together. Peter then asked, "What do they call Mister Clifton?"" A snicker came from behind. It was the boy who had put his arm around Peter's shoulders. "Biffy!" he smiled broadly. "We call him Biffy." he answered.

Peter looked horrified. His face paled when he asked, "Is it Biffy cuz he hits ya?""

"Naaa, nothing like that." the suitcase boy answered, "It's Biffy cuz all the kids call him that behind his back. Don't ask why. It's just that.... that....damn it, his nickname's Biffy, that's all. But watch it," the boy cautioned, "when he calls you by your last name. He's pissed at you."

The New Johnnies gathered in one large room where lockers lined the walls. Each boy busily emptied his suitcase and for the moment Peter felt tense; the narrow locker was now his life. He barely managed to reach the hooks anchored to each side of the inner locker and finally hung his clothes on them. When he turned Mister Clifton had taken a position directly behind him. Do you have enough room, Peter Pappas?" he asked.

The boy looked into the wry, smiling face of the adult. The man's penetrating eyes were looking beyond the boy where they were fixed on the meager belongings hanging in the locker. "Yes sir, Mister Clifton." he answered quickly.

"And these are the only clothes you own?" his brow knit into a frown.

"Yes sir, Mister Clifton."

The Instructor's eyes met those of the confused youngster, "Well, I guess they'll have to do for the time being, young man."

Peter draped a pair of pants over a wooden bar in the locker. A dark red sweater lay on the top shelf along with two pairs of stockings, a set of still packaged underwear and a box of mints. On each of the two hooks were a wrinkled dress shirt and one frayed lumberman's shirt. On the floor of the locker a pair of worn sneakers displayed holes made by his little toes.

The blood drained from Peter's face when he quickly explained, "My father will be sending me new clothes, Mister Clifton, just as soon as he gets some extra money, Sir." Suddenly, his cheeks flushed which proved it was a tell-tale lie.

Minutes later all the New Johnnies were gathered at the rear of the huge Bulfinch building. Clifton stood at the foot of a walk which led to a quadrangle of buildings, three of which were still in a state of construction. The adult explained, "Boys, in a few months you'll be moving into these new dormitories. Since they're not finished yet, you'll be sleeping in the dormitory at the top floor of Bulfinch."

Peter looked up the side of the building. A small bird flit from one window to another and then it flew away. The twelve year old's eyes betrayed his confusion, while the Instructor continued to explain that the fourth building in the quadrangle was where they would find the dining room.

"There's....There's no fire escape, Mister Clifton." The youth interrupted.

Clifton's eyebrows shot up questioningly, "What are you talking about, Peter?"

An open youthful face stared back in alarm. As if on cue the other boys stepped back, leaving the twelve year old alone in the center of their circle. Peter licked his lips, then repeated while pointing toward the top of the massive building, "There's no fire escape, Mister Clifton."

"No fire escape?" Clifton asked. "You mean you didn't see a fire escape. Isn't that right, Pappas?"

The warning about Clifton using the last name came clamoring into the boy's mind. "I want you to go by that tennis court and look up the side of the building and return to me." The adult's voice was stern. Peter took halting steps. He felt the eyes of his fellow students riveted on himself. But, he did not care for he remembered it was a five story red-bricked building, very much like Bulfinch, when Yia Yia's terrified yells awoke everyone. The fifth floor apartment was full of smoke.

Peter clutched Anna where they slept in the same bed as Yia Yia Fear filled them when the old lady demanded obedience from the older brothers. Windows were smashed for they could not be opened on that frigid December night. The six year old twins were bundled in frightened flight and carried down wooden stairs - there was no fire escape.

When Peter arrived at the tennis court he was shocked to see not one, but two massive fire escapes secured at that end of the building. He turned and slowly walked back to the group with his eyes fixed on the ground. With his hands jammed into his pants pockets he wondered how much trouble he had gotten himself into.

At that moment Clifton said, "Come along boys, it's time for your lunch." A creeping contented smile crossed the adult's lips when he placed his arm around Peter's shoulders and said, "I like a boy who's not afraid to speak up when things bother him." Peter simply smiled with relief.

The new boys grouped together where they followed Mister Clifton in the direction of the dining room. Peter still felt uncomfortable with his earlier confrontation with the Instructor. He was always shy. He would be the last to speak if things really bothered, but today, for some unknown reason, he let his feelings be known.

And what was it his brother Lou said to him that morning at City Point before he boarded the boat. "Go out there and be a king." Yea, sure! He took closer look at the other boys in the group, now mentally measuring his own height to them, only to be disappointed that he looked rather puny in comparison.

A voice suddenly spoke from behind when it said, "You really stepped in a pile of shit with Clifton, didn't-cha?" Peter turned instantly when he faced another of the New johnnies. He was a bit taller than Peter, a boy with a pronounced limp in his left leg, where his left shoe barely rose off the ground. "What?" Peter asked in surprise.

"Don't let them bug ya. We're all gonna screw up some time."

The younger Peter felt challenged when his shoulders stiffened then instantly relaxed where his fellow New Johnnie warmed up a smile and said, "My name's Benson." He breathed heavily, a raspy sound coming from his throat, "And you?" he asked.

"Pappas." the younger boy snapped trying to act tough.

"And what's this crap about fire escapes?" He clapped a friendly hand on Peter's shoulder.

"Oh, it's just that I like being called Petee. Everyone at home calls me Petee." Bright blue eyes looked up into the sallow face of his new found friend.

"And the fire escape?" the boy pressed the issue.

Peter's brow tightened into a frown when he answered,

"When I was six our apartment house caught fire. It was December and freezing cold. We lived on the fifth floor. There was no fire escape. We were lucky we all got out."

"Did-ja get yourself killed?" Ralph asked facetiously.

Peter threw up his hands in disbelief, "No Benson." he giggled, "I wouldn't be here if I got killed." Benson flashed a sly, amused smile, he then said, "It's okay Petee. If that's what you want to be called, that's what I'll call you and you can call me Ralph." He gave the boy a short mischievous smile

CHAPTER TWO

THE PEANUT LADY

It was late evening when the new boys were ushered up the five flights of steep stairs to the dormitories. Peter gripped the railing and hauled himself up, occasionally peeking over to view the abyss created by the winding stairs. Suspended from somewhere at the roof a long thick roped dangled all the way to the first floor. "I wonder what that rope's for?" he asked the boy next to him. "I dunno. Maybe you slide down if there's a 'mergency. The answer was quick.

Peter looked confused. His eyes were riveted as far up into the mysteriously dark belfry. "Do ya really think so?" he asked incredulously. "Well, I ain't gonna slide down any rope, 'mergency or no 'mergency."

Suddenly, a voice from somewhere above said, "It pulls the fire bell in case of fire, you dimwits."

When they entered the spacious dormitory they looked in amazement where the massive room was filled with beds and instructed that there were enough beds in the middle row for each new student. Clifton guided them in their selection and then pointed to a half walled enclosure that would be the only toilet they would use should they need it during the night. Once the boys selected their beds he announced, "Under your pillow you'll find a nightshirt" His voice rose authoritatively, "You will wear the nightshirt. We do not allowe pajamas."

Peter squirmed onto his bed, his finger probed under the pillow. He tugged the white nightshirt until a portion of it was exposed and then pushed it back quickly. It had been a long time since he wore pajamas. Ever since Yia Yia died he slept in his shorts. He never heard of a nightshirt and wondered what it was used for. The clock over the door read eight-fifty, the corners of the boy's mouth turned down somberly, for at home he never went to bed before ten. Of course, when Yia Yia was alive it was a different story.

He undressed slowly while watching the other boys do the same thing. It was very quiet in the large room except for the shuffling of clothes and shoes striking the floor. He had removed his shirt and then sat quietly on the bed before removing his pants. He hesitated because he did not want anyone to see his filthy shorts for he had to get rid of them without anyone seeing him and he fretted over how he would do it.

But, getting rid of them would have to wait, he now faced the problem of putting on his nightshirt. When he thought everyone's attention was focused on Clifton he dropped his pants and quickly slipped the cumbersome gown over his head, then let the hem fall to his shins. His mind raced at the thought he was now wearing a dress, a very long dress. He hated it. But then, he caught sight of his friend Benson struggling with his gown and he snickered to himself.

Casting a wary eye at Mister Clifton he had this feeling the Instructor was staring right at him. "He saw them! Mister Clifton must have seen my shorts. My filthy shorts." His thoughts raced with his embarrassment. "He was looking right at me and I know he saw my shorts." The thought hung tenaciously. Finally, he slipped under the covers and with his momentum the nightshirt slipped up to his waist. Disturbed and uncomfortable he struggled to pull it down, now wriggling like a stranded eel. Finding it useless to pursue gripping the damnable dress he lay back and stared thoughtfully into space. He now knew where he would be sleeping tonight. Clifton abruptly left the huge chamber.

Suddenly, a burst of voices filled the doorway. Crowded together a large group of older boys jostled each other in playful contests to see who would get through the door first. "Hey, New Johnnies!" A voice filled the room. The new boys looked anxiously at their older schoolmates. "I hope none of you guys snore." Another voice brought cat-calls which echoed in the vast dormitory.

It seemed like bedlam to Peter who lay with his hands tucked under his head while the bellicose young men found their beds and quickly undressed. "Anyone piss the bed and you'll be washing your own sheets tomorrow." A voice shouted from the other end of the room. An explosion of laughter brought spasms of guffaws.

Peter smiled at the silliness. They reminded him of how his four older brothers often behaved as badly only to have the petite Yia Yia admonish them all. When he had the measles they swarmed onto his bed and overwhelmed him with a flurry of excitement and frenzy. They too were loud and mischievous, tickling his feet while another held him down until he begged for mercy. It was always Yia Yia who came to his rescue, shooing the offending brothers away.

Suddenly, a man's voice shouted above the din. "Everyone stand at the foot of your beds." Silence instantly filled the room. He wore a leather jacket which accented large shoulders. A pencil-thin moustache had been precisely clipped on an oval face. His blue and gold baseball cap was emblazoned with the initials FTS. It lay crushed and ill fitting on his head where brown curly hairs stood out starkly from the sides.

A leather strap crossed his chest from his shoulder where it held a bulging round clock that dangled at his hip. The cavernous room was suddenly plunged into darkness. Peter stood nervously at the end of his bed along with the others. He felt a shiver of excitement rush through him for this was something new. He filled his head with thoughts of punishment, truly the result of the older boys making too much noise.

The stillness was eerie. Scores of nightshirts looked ghostly where the early moon cast a dull glow through the windows. Suddenly, sharp, crisp notes from a trumpet startled the boy. Punctuated notes blended into a soft refrain of taps. The large chamber echoed with the melodic tune. The twelve year old had never heard taps before. He wondered what it all meant... Finally, the resonant notes ended with the last long spooky note.

As if on cue the boys slid under their sheets. The youngster tugged the end of his nightshirt and pushed it toward his ankles, now more determined to keep the hem where it belonged at his ankles.

With one mighty shove he slid himself between his sheets only to have the gown slide up to his waist again. He gave up trying to control it and vowed never to tell his twin sister Anna that he had to wear a white dress to bed.

From the corner, directly to Peter's left, the toilet flushed. Water swirled noisily when a raucous rush seemed to run endlessly when it refilled the holding tank. A nightgown crossed in front of Peter's bed. Plodding feet hustled to the far end of the room. A squeak of a bedspring and the twelve year old knew someone found his bed.

The boy waited until he heard the others breathing in sleep. He slipped out of his bed and knelt beside it. It was a long prayer his Yia Yia had him learn and he said it every night; sleep would be impossible if he neglected this ritual. When he finally crawled into bed he suddenly became acutely aware of new sounds in the dorm. He pictured a bat or a bird flying in the huge room.

Swishing sounds conjured up pictures of an eagle flying close to the ceiling and then he knew it it would dive headlong and attack him and tear the flesh off his face. He peeked from under the covers and squinted far into the darkness, far into the recesses of an unfamiliar massive room, but it was useless. It was impossible to even see the ghostly light from the moon.

The swishing sound he heard was now more intense as anxiety slowly overcame him. Blue eyes blinked at the ceiling while his mouth set resolutely - waiting anxiously for something to happen. When tucking his head under the covers he suddenly realized the sounds were coming from the beds that surrounded him. It was the boys! It was the boys turning in their beds and their bodies rubbing the sheets that made the swishing sounds. Now drowsy and content that he solved the mystery he drifted off to sleep.

A blast from a trumpet shredded every one of Peter's nerves. He sat bolt upright when his brain now dulled from sleep screamed at him to wake up instantly. His nightshirt had crawled up to his shoulders and he tried hopelessly to pull the cumbersome shirt down. In that anxious moment the staccato notes of reveille echoed. Howls from the older boys scolded the bugler, but it was all in fun. The boy saw the man with the blue and gold cap standing by the door next to the youth with the trumpet. The round clock was still suspended at his waist.

"Alright, you guys." he raised his voice, "On your feet. Get dressed. Beds made. I want you out of here in ten minutes."

"Who's he?" Peter asked his neighbor.

"I don't know." The other new boy answered, "But he sure looks mean." The two boys eyed the man critically, youthful glances held an edge of suspense.

Peter rushed to make his bed by copying the methods of the older boys. No matter how he tried it still looked unmade. A line quickly formed by the single commode, the twelve year old knew he could never hold himself that long.

"Come on! Come on! Everybody out!" The man shouted at the boys. "Take care of your bathroom needs downstairs.."

The youngster started to remove his nightshirt when he remembered he was still wearing his dirty shorts. Casting a quick look at the others who were busy dressing to meet the time limit, he hoped he had finally found his one chance slip out of his offensive shorts. In one motion he pulled them off and jammed them under his arm pit so his shirt hid them.

Peter rushed to the adult. "Sir, is there a bathroom downstairs?" he asked desperately, his face now contorted with his urgency. The stern night watchman smiled down at the squirming boy, "On the first floor, lad. Off the assembly room." Peter raced down the five flights, ran into the assembly room only to crash headlong into Mister Clifton. The anguished boy looked up at the startled adult and asked breathlessly, "The toilet, sir? The man smiled tightly, then pointed to a door at the far end of the room. Peter forgot to thank him, but it did not matter, this was an emergency. When finished, the youngster crammed the offensive shorts deep into a trash barrel and left the room.

It was but a few minutes later when the assembly room filled with the full student body down from the dormitory. They formed three lines with the youngest and shortest at the front row. Two hundred boys lined up in formation, their toes successively meeting scored lines in the cement floor.

A man stood at the front with a clipboard under his arm. Deep scowling eyes scanned the room. When he squinted his brow knit up menacingly. Finally, he blew a shrill whistle and the room instantly quieted. Peter winced from the piercing whistle, then eyed the man warily. Finally, the adult cast a searching look at the New Johnnies, then spoke in a monotone. "For you New Johnnies, I'm Mister Donlevy. I'm your supervisor." His eyes were momentarily fixed on each new boy. "You'll report here four times a day for roll call." Gray colored eyes chilled the youngsters, "Before breakfast, lunch, supper and bed." he continued.

Peter looked in awe when the instructions were given. He stood positively still, not daring to let his toes cross the line. His heartbeat pulsed loudly in his ears, it always happened when sharp noises caught him by surprise just like when it happened with the bugler in the dorm. The whistle was too shrill and cutting. If hammers pounded nails the noise would force his eyelids to blink with each strike. Fire sirens found him cupping his hands over his ears.

"You there!" Donlevy's voice rose in a rage. He jabbed his pen at the back row. "Do you find this assembly funny?" he snapped. He glared at some culprit in the back. A pulsating vein stuck out from the side of the Instructor's neck. It was then the twelve year old noticed a mottled scar which ran from the back of his ear, then disappeared behind his shirt collar. A round, thick lipped face glared over the heads of the smaller boys.

"Come up to the front." he demanded.

Peter heard shuffling from behind. He dared not look, but kept his face to the front, his eyes riveted on Donlevy. A thin, red headed student appeared off to the left. He stood with his feet apart, his hands clasped behind him. He casually looked up at the ceiling and slowly rocked back and forth on his heels. Finally, his eyes fell on the disciplinarian.

"What's so funny, Pasko?" Donlevy stood directly in front of the youth, his hands clamped on his hips like a drill sergeant. Now inches from the tight-lipped teenager's face he snarled, "Well, speak to me!"

The muted answer said, "Nothing, sir."

Peter's eyes were crammed to the left, his head pointed front. For an instant his gaze locked with that of Pasko. He was a tall, thin student with frizzy red hair curled tightly on his head. His shirt and pants were laced like a corrugated box, deep creases ran in different directions. He had outgrown kahki pants for the legs of his trousers ended at his ankles. Scuffed black brogans cupped his ankles, laces flopped untied.

There was a tenseness in the big room. Peter felt uneasy when his face suddenly flushed crimson. It happened often when he pitied someone else.

"I'm giving you a demerit!" Donlevy snapped. "Now get back in line!"

Peter's riveted stare followed the grim faced Instructor who repositioned himself before the group. Pasko retreated hastily to the rear. "Does anyone else think something's funny?" The voice echoed in the barren room. Peter's mind raced to Donlvey's remark, "I'm giving you a demerit!" The youngster's brow furrowed questioningly when he asked himself, "What's a demerit?"

For you New Johnnies," Donlevy continued in a monotone, "breakfast is at seven. Lunch is twelve noon sharp and supper is at six. If you miss any of these meals you better have a damn excuse." His piercing glare searched out each boy individually. "You will report at exactly half past six in the morning, at half past eleven at noon and at half past five before supper. At night you'll report at half past eight for roll call." His words cut like a knife when he added, "Are there any questions?" There were none. "Everyone's dismissed except the New Johnnies." he announced.

Twenty young boys stood breathlessly at attention. From behind, shuffling shoes merged toward the back door. A subdued sense of abandon accompanied the withdrawing older students. Donlevy positioned himself in front of the first boy in line and asked his name. "Rholf Swenson, Sir." A high pitched voice answered.

James Whitemore, Sir." A second voice followed.

"Rene LaBlanc, Sir." And then in rapid order the others followed, "Chester MacDougal, Sir. Paul Burns, Sir. Isaiah Feldman, Sir. Ralph Benson, Sir." Petee Pappas, Sir. Samuel Kent, Sir."

Hold it!" Donlevy interrupted. His face pinched in a frown. He then asked the terrified twelve year old, "What did you say your name was?"

The boy gulped nervously. His eyes were fixed on the man's rigid glare. "Petee Pappas, S-S-Sir," he stammered. He knew he goofed again, but calling himself Petee was a habit he could not shake. His heart beat thunderously when he waited for the reprimand.

Donlevy frowned down at the small boy. "Petee?" the Instructor asked. "That doesn't sound like a name to me, young fella." Suddenly, he clapped his hands together, a resounding thwack filled the room. Peter arched backward and away from the threat. Finally, a controlled voice demanded, "Tell me your real name and cut out the crap. Do you understand?" He leaned forward, now towering over the petrified youngster.

"I'm....I'm Peter Pappas, Sir." The boy's voice was barely audible when he tried to stifle a sob. His nostrils immediately began to drain and he tried with all his might not to sniffle, but it was no use, he just had to make a sound he could not stop. Donlevy's voice dropped an octave when he leaned close to the boy's face and snarled, "I don't like wise punks. Do you hear me, kid?" He did not wait for an answer, but dismissed the boys for breakfast.

The New Johnnies walked across the quadrangle. A subdued group, yet, somewhat disconnected from Peter. Ralph Benson, the boy with the profound limp walked next to Peter and remarked callously, "It looks like Donlevy's a real bastard, don't you think?"

The twelve year old looked at the taller Benson and saw the comment was directed at him. Peter silently hunched his shoulders, then shoved his hands into his pockets. He sneaked a quick look at Benson's awkward limp in his right leg. The taller boy had to struggle to keep up with the others.

"I guess I screwed up, huh?" Pappas whispered conspiratorially.

"Why'd ya tell him your name's Petee, fer chrise-sake?" he asked when the group came to a halt outside the dining room building. "When he slapped his hands together I thought sure in hell he cracked you across the face."

The youngster suddenly realized the others had stopped their chatter and were waiting for an answer. "I dunno." Peter replied, "It slipped out." A voice from the edge of the group snapped, "I hope he doesn't take it out on all of us on account of you." Peter looked up impulsively. A sea of anxious faces glared at him. Ralph Benson placed his arm around the boy's shoulders and said, "It's okay, Pappas. They know you're new here and you don't know the ropes." Peter gave him a quick, nervous smile of relief, "You seem to know a lot about the school?" the boy asked.

The reply was quick and cutting, "Been to enough of 'em." Suddenly Mister Clifton arrived and formed them into a line for their table assignments.

It was later that afternoon when all the new boys were each handed their own towel, then ordered to strip their clothes off . Peter looked horrified when Clifton added, "We expect you to shower often. Now don't' be shy." The Instructor smiled unpretentiously when the boys slowly slipped out of their garments. The twelve year old hesitated for this was the very first time he ever undressed in public. He gulped nervously, then took his clothes and held them in front of him while nude bodies of his classmates passed silently by. Everyone's eyes were fixed on the cascading water spurting from jets in another room. Steam formed a mist that felt it was sucking his breath away.

Suddenly, he was nudged from behind when a smiling Ralph Benson asked jokingly, "Betcha nobody's seen your balls before, eh, Petee?" he teased.

The humiliated youngster looked at the limping boy and asked, "What?"

"I've been to other places like this, Petee. Everybody's ball-shy at first." he snickered.

Peter smiled impishly, "Ball-shy?" he asked. "Yea! Looka them there. They got their asses stickin out like flags." He smirked suggestively and continued, "Not one of 'em's got their eyes on anybody's crotch. They're all looking at the ceiling like they're praying."

Benson led the way where torrents of water poured over the two of them. The deluge forced Peter to shut his eyes for a moment. When he faced Benson again he giggled and repeated, "Ball-shy."

It was almost evening when the sun's rays turned the harbor waters into a glimmering iridescent rainbow. Sailboats cut across the tops of waves like bobbing sailfish, their prow cut cleanly toward a distant mooring. The New Johnnies had gathered under a giant elm tree which stood next to the Bulfinch building's assembly room. Surrounding the massive trunk a wooden bench had recently been painted for the warning signs of "WET PAINT" forced the boys to sit on the cement walk while they waited.

"You're going to meet the Peanut Lady, boys." Clifton flashed a warm smile at the teenagers. His eyebrows arched in mock surprise when he asked, "Don't you believe me?" The boys giggled in anticipation. Curious grins met the suspicious announcement. Finally, a youngster asked, "Mister Clifton, Sir. Are there any wild 'animals on the island?

Clifton pursed his lips and answered, "The only wild animals on this island are you guys."

"Someone told us there's a ghost that lives in the cemetery at the south end of the island." Inquisitive eyes fell upon the Instructor, "They said the ghost guards the shore so noneof the kids can escape." The boy frowned and held his breath for an answer.

Clifton threw his hands up in disbelief. His eyes bulged behind his glasses when he at first stiffened in false surprise and then warmed into a gentle smile. "Son, I've lived on this island for twenty-four years. If there's a ghost, I haven't seen it."

Ralph Benson nudged Peter and urged, "Go ahead, Petee Ask him." The twelve year old took a quick look at his friend, then cast a fearful eye at the Instructor. "Go ahead, Petee. Ask him." Benson persisted. Finally, the youngster found his courage and asked, "Mister Clifton, Sir, is there really a cemetery out on the south end of the island where they bury kids. Like if we die? -1 mean...." He scratched his cheek nervously.

Clifton burst into laughter. He looked at the Bulfinch Building which was now awash in the sun's fading rays. Turning back he answered with a chuckle, "Young man, the cemetery hasn't been used in fifty years. Once there was an orphanage on this island and yes, if a boy died he was buried in our own cemetery. But they don't do that today" He grinned at the innocence of the questioner. Peter cringed since all eyes had fallen upon him.

"Okay everyone. We've a ways to go. Let's get moving." The adult led the group down a gently sloping hill where they proceeded along a dirt road leading through an orchard. Smells of rotting fruit found a few spindly branches that held but a few apples and pears that were in stages of decay since the season had long past, yet an apple fragrance continued to linger over the orchard.

"We're heading toward the south end. Peter whispered with an edge of excitement in his voice, "D'ya think Mister Clifton's taking us to the cemetery?"

Benson was exasperated when he snapped, "Petee, Clifton said we're going to see a peanut lady or something, that's all. So forget this bullshit about ghosts, will ya?"

The youngster clapped his hand over his mouth when an idea struck him, "Yea, but, what's a peanut lady doin' where there ain't no buildings?

Hey, Ralph," his voice held a tremor of fear. "What if she's the ghost?" Large questioning eyes focused on his handicapped friend. But Benson was having trouble of his own keeping pace with the others and soon lagged far behind. Peter, now preoccupied with his fantasy failed to see what was happening. The group of New Johnnies continued to follow Clifton. There was a chill in the September night. In the distance ocean waves broke noisily on shore, but they were hidden by the embankment. But still, the frothy bubbles made by the breaking waves hissed like escaping steam.

"I heard there's rats on the island, Ralph."

Benson's breathing was more labored when he asked, "Common, Petee. Who told you that?"

"Some of the big guys were talking that the dogs are trained to kill rats."

"Dogs don't kill rats." Irritation had built in Ralph's voice. He was annoyed with the twelve year old and his childish fears.

"Oh yea! Well, I heard them say some of the rats is as big as cats and that's why they ain't got no cats on the island."

"Petee! For chrise-sakes, shut up!" Benson's exasperation caught the younger boy by surprise. "If you keep this scary stuff up they're gonna put you in the funny farm. They'll probably lock you in the basement of Bulfinch." He finally caught his breath and the two lingerers tried to catch up to the others.

Oddly, Peter suddenly became very quiet. He looked back at the massive building possessing the top of the hill. A setting sun cast an ominous pall over the columned structure. The youngster's lips tightened. He looked concerned. Could Ralph know something about putting kids in the basement of Bulfinch? A troubled gaze appeared in his eyes when he pictured rusted cages in dark, damp dungeons. His imagination raced when he envisioned walls laced with spider webs. Eerie, fleshy, slim legged Black Widow spiders crouched ominously, ready to spring at him.

"What's the matter, Petee?" Ralph asked with some concern over the boy's distant mood.

Peter did not want to be laughed at about his fears of the Bulfinch basement. He simply answered, "I gotta go to the bathroom."

Ralph pointed to a tree, "So piss behind that tree." He thought he resolved the problem matter-of-factly.

Peteer's nose wrinkled distastefully, "I don't have to pee, Ralph." He chewed his bottom lip nervously. "You know what I mean. I haven't gone since we came to this school."

"What!." Ralph looked shocked, "You ain't taken a shit since three days ago?"

"It's that big toilet, Ralph. Every time I sit down someone comes in and I get all nervous. There's too many hoppers, ya know?"

"Jeezus, Petee, you ain't ball shy, so why are ya ass shy?"

The boy shrugged his shoulders and kicked the ground with his shoe, "I'll.....I'll try and go tonight." he answered hopefully.

"Cripes, they'll be giving you an enema and you won't like that cuz I've had them and they ain't no fun."

Blue eyes looked up in fright, "What's a nemena?

"They shove this thing up your ass and they fill you with stuff and you feel like you're gonna explode." the knowledgeable friend explained, "And then, when you take a crap they stand there and watch you, Petee, so's they make sure it all comes out."

The boy paled. His jaw dropped open. Finally, through trembling lips he defended, "Well, no one's giving me no nemena. I'm gonna make sure I go tonight."

They had lagged so far behind the others who had already reached their destination. Finally catching up they entered a small grove of trees which gave way to a large white farm house awash in a friendly moon's embrace. Everyone had assembled on the back porch when the door opened abruptly.

She was a diminutive woman whose hair was wrapped in a red and white polka dot kerchief which accented her ebony skin. Dark brown eyes unflinchingly stirred a gaze, faltering at first until they adjusted to the cobalt moon which danced its beams between the leafy trees. She studied each new boy with what seemed troubled eyes and when she focused on Peter he hastily sucked in his breath. He whispered to Ralph, "She looks like a witch."

Benson poked him in the ribs with his elbow and snapped, "Damn it, Petee. Stop talking like that."

Clifton's voice rose in the night when he announced, "Boys, this is the peanut lady."

The petite woman warmed up a gentle smile, "Welcome to our school, boys." Her melodic voice flowed like a delicate breeze. When she stepped back she pointed to a huge, bulging burlap sack off to her right. She then instructed that the boys take two handful of peanuts and fill their pockets, remembering to take only that which they would eat.

The boys surrounded the clumsy sack. Small hands clutched each fistful of the shell covered treats. Peter avoided passing directly in front of the lady, but rather circled the outer edge of the other boys who were filling their pockets with the peanuts. He cast a foreboding eye at his hostess who was now speaking with Mister Clifton.

Peter filled his pockets then stepped warily away where he casually observed the petite lady drumming her fingers on crossed arms while speaking to the Instructor. A small porch ceiling light cast her shadow on an opposite wall which enlarged the darkened image of her kerchief shaping it like a bat. The twelve year old lips moved imperceptibly when he agreed with himself that for certain the lady was indeed a witch.

The boys followed Clifton where he led them along the dirt road. Peanut shells were crushed by nimble fingers, everyone chewed nosily. Once within a small grove of trees they burst onto the open shore. Gentle ocean waves curled the seaside then fractured a torrent of tiny bubbles that sounded like a million hissing snakes.

The Instructor was seated on a log, surrounded by the adventurous students who eagerly awaited the next phase of their introduction to the island school. In moments school songs were memorized and the vocalizing youths filled the cool night air with the intoxicating melodies.

Peter was seated in a front row with his friend Benson directly at his right elbow. There was a lull in the singing when the youngster asked, "Mister Clifton, Sir. Is the peanut lady a witch?" A dramatic hush suddenly fell over the others. Clifton stared steadily at the boy, then burst into laughter. He then answered, "Why you know better than that, Pappas." The boy grimaced at the use of his last name. He knew he had angered the adult. Benson elbowed his friend at the ridiculous question. The boy looked anxiously at the Instructor, then returned an uneasy smile. His face now flushed when a torrent of giggles from the other boys filled the night. Clifton asked, "Do you think she's a witch, young man?" Peter shrugged his shoulders hoping this would satisfy as an answer. He wished he had never brought the subject up.

"What makes you think she's a witch?" Clifton continued the encounter.

Peter met Clifton's stony glare, then the boy's gaze faltered. He felt the stares of his fellow students who continued to giggle. "Cuz she looks like a witch, Sir." He answered awkwardly.

Clifton leaned forward for it was time he taught all the students a serious lesson. His brow wrinkled into a a silent frown. His voice was stern and commanding, "No adult on this island is ever to be called a witch. Miss Pederson lives at the old farm house because she is a botanist. Do you know what a botanist is? He aimed his question at Peter who shrugged his shoulders again, only this time he lowered his eyes in embarrassment. "A botanist is someone who studies plants." Clifton continued, "Miss Pederson works for the University of Massachusetts and is here studying island plant life. She's doing what is called research." His eyebrows raised questioningly. "Do you understand me?"

Peter shifted his legs nervously. He knew he was the one to give the answer for all the New Johnnies. He felt his face turning red from the attention that was focused on him. "Yes, Sir." He answered sheepishly.

Clifton immediately changed the mood when he asked for another song. He patted the twelve year old on the head and then whispered so only the boy could hear, "A witch? You must be a nut." He winked at the boy and the tension fell away. His friend Ralph placed an arm around this shattered friend, "I guess you stepped in another pile of shit that time, Petee." He squeezed the boy's shoulder while the youngster made circles in the sand with his finger. The younger boy then said, "They call him Biffy." He squirreled his nose in regret that he let the nickname slip out, but it was the only way he could retaliate at being admonished in front of his classmates.

Benson looked surprised, "Who they call Biffy?" A small round chin jutted at Clifton. Ralph's voice rose in excitement, "Clifton's called Biffy?" Peter looked up in alarm. His eyes flashed to Mister Clifton who was talking to the group and obviously distracted from the two who were speaking secretly. "SHUSH! SHUSH!" Peter pleaded. "I should'na told you."

CHAPTER THREE

AN ACCIDENT WAITING

It was later in the Fall, shortly after classes had begun when Peter and Ralph sneaked away to the hay barn where they climbed far into the hay loft. They crawled through the dry winter's hay which was piled precipitously close to the lofty ceiling. The sheer height gave the two boys a scary view which descended to the main wooden floor, now covered with large farm equipment so far below. Peter blinked several times where he lay fascinated with the view.

"What's hay smell like to you, Petee?" Ralph asked when he turned on his back and stared up at the ceiling which was only a few scary feet away.

A wrinkled nose met the question when Ralph's friend answered, "It's kinda sweet, ain't it, Ralph? It's like....like a buncha dried leaves." The boy pushed his face into the hay and took a deep smell.

The barn reeked with several odors which blended in a balance of disharmony. Horses on the first floor prompted the smell of manure, while fifty head of Guernsey cows on the floor below the horses sent waves of warm hide-sweat far up to the ceiling, plus a different smell from their manure. It was a mixture filled with damp, ocean humidity and so many other farm smells couched under the blanket of wood which framed the barn.

"Ya know, Petee, " Ralph whispered, "we could get a big demerit for being up here."

"We'll have at sneak around, huh Ralph? It's Sunday and nobody's working."

The boys continued to play in the hay. They tossed hands full of the dried fodder at each other while squirming like moles into the hay only to find it was packed too tightly to make a hole. Finally, Peter raised his head, tangled strands of his hair were filled with scraggly cow feed. The boy's eyes focused on his friend who lay on his back while grasping the hay and tossing it in the air where it landed aimlessly over his body. For a moment Ralph was miles away in thought while he continued to toss the feed automatically into the air.

"Hey Ralph? Peter asked innocently, "How come ya don't use a cane when you walk? I mean you walk with a limp and all that? It'll help ya, won't it?"

Benson stopped tossing the hay. A firm tightness contracted the muscles in his face. He continued to stare high into the rafters when he finally snapped, "Why don't you mind your own god-damned business, Petee?" Peter looked aghast. His lower lip trembled when his mouth dropped open. He squirmed uncomfortably in the hay with his eyes fixed on his friend. He realized he had blundered into something so personal.

"I....I didn't mean it that way, Ralph." He felt shattered that he offended his friend. Searching his mind he tried frantically to ease the awkward situation. Tears were held back when he blurted in a sob, "I guess I said the wrong thing, huh, Ralph?"

The handicapped boy did not answer. He continued to stare blankly at the rafters which crisscrossed the roof of the barn. Peter buried his face into his hands. Tears washed his palms when he tried with all of his might to hold back the sounds of crying. In a flash he suddenly heard the crunch of hay. Before he could take his hands away from his face he felt the full force of Ralph's body drop on top of him. "Ralph!" the boy shrieked in fright. "I didn't mean it." Fear gripped his very soul.

"Making fun of me, eh, Petee." The bigger boy straddled the youngster, he then bounced up and down on the immobilized Peter. A screech filled the barn when the twelve year old tried to extricate himself - it was hopeless. Ralph leaned close and snarled, "This'll teach ya to make fun of your best friend." He continued to jostle the bewildered youth and then pulled him by the shoulders until Peter lay flat on his back. Ralph continued to sit on the boy.

When Peter opened his eyes he saw his friend smiling down on him. "You ain't mad at me?" Peter's voice cracked with emotion. Ralph did not answer, but lay over him and pinned the youth's arms above his head. "Now you've got to rassle me, Petee. And the winner," he pointed to himself, "is gonna make the loser his slave for a week." He slid off the prostrated youth and crawled on all fours, then waited at the side.

Peter struggled to position himself, "You ain't gonna make me your slave, Ralph Benson." He snarled contemptuously. The two lunged at each other until flaying arms wrapped around each body. The heavier Ralph immediately had the advantage when he tossed his friend over his shoulders. The boy landed with a splat into loose hay, but instantly turned and charged his adversary. Losing his footing in the slippery hay Peter crawled on all fours, then waited at the side; clothes were covered with dried grass.

Ralph grinned like a demon when he charged his friend who was bobbing right and left anticipating the pounding he was about to take. In a flash Ralph smothered the younger boy with his body and then pulled clumps of hay from the loft and shoved it into his face. Peter gagged from the dust, then coughed violently when trying to clear his lungs. Ralph slid off to the side to let the youngster catch his breath.

Undaunted with the spasms, Peter knew he had the advantage of surprise when he pounced on the startled Ralph who took the brunt of the jolt and twisted to his left. Now distracted Ralph did not realize he was perilously close to the edge of the loft. The slippery hay offered him no traction when suddenly he screamed in terror when he fell from the upper tier, tumbling with hands clawing the air. Thirty feet below a sickening thud met Peter's horrified gaze.

"RALPH!" Peter shrieked at the unbelievable sight and there groans from below met the concerned yells from his horrified friend.

Scampering down a ladder Peter screamed at the frightful scene where his friend lay face down on the hard wooden barn floor. Waves of horror swept the approaching Peter who stood riveted in fear. Rushing to the huge open barn doors he frantically searched for help, but there was no one around. Turning he and shouted, "Ralph! I didn't mean it. Ralph....Ralph can you hear me? I.... didn't mean it."

Kneeling next to his friend trembling hands touched the injured youth's shoulder when suddenly Benson's eyes flicked open. An empty stare met Peter's wide-eyed look of despair. Suddenly, Ralph gripped Peter's hand and squeezed It tightly when a sharp twinge of pain seized him. "I....I'm hurting, Petee." His voice was hollow. He grit his teeth tightly when he got to his knees and slowly rose to his feet. "I'll go get help." Peter begged as he helped the boy steady himself.

"No!" Ralph snapped, "Don't tell anyone this happened. It's my ribs, Petee. They hurt bad, but I don't think they're broken." Ever so slowly they left the barn. Ralph draped his arm on Peter's shoulders and slowly started up the hill toward the administration building.

It was an arduous climb, however, their only thought was of the demerit they were certain to get for going out of bounds without permission Arriving at the top of the hill a man's voice called out to them. Two hearts sank as one. Ralph, with difficulty, tried to straighten his clothes and faced the on-coming adult. A stern look of disapproval was etched on the red haired Couches face. The two offenders stared back helplessly when the rugged athletic director eyed their disheveled appearance. They knew that hay was clinging to their clothes and there would be no way to hide it from him. But hiding Ralph's injury was another problem they had to face. Could they pull it off. Only time would tell.

"Where have you guy's been?" the Coach snapped when his penetrating eyes looked them up and down.

Peter knew the truth would eventually come out when he answered coyly. " We were in the barn, Coach Johnson.

The burly man eyed Ralph suspiciously and asked "And what are you hiding, Benson? Why are you rubbing your ribs" He looked at the boy with stony disapproval.

The answer was quick. "Bumped my ribs, sir."

"Have you guys been fighting?"

"Oh no Sir." The twelve year old answered quickly, "Me and Ralph's friends."

The red headed coach eyed them suspiciously when he walked away and said over his shoulder, "I want to see the two of you in my cubicle before supper." Peter gulped nervously. He glanced at Ralph who continued to clutch his ribs. They knew a visit to the cubicle meant trouble, a demerit or worse, maybe having to work all their free time. This was the first time Peter or Ralph had to report to the cubicle and as sinister as it sounded, they knew from what the other boys had told them that nothing good ever came out of the cubicle.

Benson tried to dismiss the incident when another sharp pain knifed into his ribs. Once again he gasped spastically for breath. Peter looked horrified when he demanded, "I'm gonna get Coach to look at you."

"NO!" Ralph snapped. He glared at his friend. An ineffectual smile crossed his lips if only to put Peter at ease.

It was before supper roll call when the two friends sat on a circular bench which surrounded a huge elm tree outside the assembly room. The Couch's cubicle was located next to the toilets in the corner. "You okay, Ralph?" Peter's concern was fixed in his eyes.

The boy shrugged him off when he asked, "I suppose Coach's gonna give us shit for being in the barn."

"Probly give us a demerit or something." The boy answered. Ralph pushed himself back into the bench to relieve the pain. He shut his eyes for a moment and said, "Ya remember that Miss Pederson down at the farm house - you remember, the peanut lady. Well, she reminds me of my mother."

Peter looked surprised when he asked, "You mean your mother's a Negro too?"

Benson looked at the boy hopelessly, "You're a god-damned jerk, Petee." He chuckled when he shook his head at the boys' naivete. But a cutting, stabbing pain cut short his amusement. In a few minutes he caught his breath and continued, "I meant my mother used to put her hair up the same way. You know, covered with a kerchief like that." He lay his head against the back of the bench and shut his eyes. Peter was unknowingly sapping his injured friend's strength when he lashed out defensively, "You swear too much, Ralph"

For some strange reason the handicapped youth suddenly brought back memories of his father. He silently brought back the day a vicious slap found him begging his father to stop, but a second blow clipped him off the ear. How the man could reach from the front seat of the car and deliver those blows was beyond his comprehension. "You little bastard." His father's voice roared, "I told you to sit still and stop kicking the back of the god-damned seat."

His Mother's scream deafened him when in that instant turmoil filled with crushing metal found the boy pinned on the floor of the car. When he stirred in the hospital bed his head ached. He could still hear his Mother's scream, but the scream blended into a train whistle while above all this the angry voice kept yelling, "You little bastard. I told you...." And then the voice suddenly stopped. He tried to turn from the oncoming slap, but, he could not move.

Suddenly, voices spoke from the foot of his bed. In a daze he heard them say his father did not see the train that hit them. With turmoil spinning in his mind the injured boy heard that someone would be walking with a limp for the rest of his life. He tried to explain he didn't have a limp, but heavy doses of pain killers found him slipping into a deep sleep. Peter's voice cut sharply into his thoughts . "Didn't-cha hear me, Ralph?"

Ralph looked confused for a moment and then he remembered Petee had said something about using too many swear words. His lips twitched into a tight, controlled smile, "I had a good teacher." He swallowed a lump in his throat, turned his head away and answered softly, "My old man never stopped swearing."

Coach Johnson suddenly appeared in the doorway, now beckoning the boys to follow him. The two miscreants took quick looks at each other then somberly followed the trainer where he led them into a small office next to the toilets - the cubicle.

The boys stood awkwardly behind the closed door. The Coach tossed his gold and blue jacket onto a chair in the corner, then sat heavily into a swivel chair in front of his desk. The chair creaked noisily when the big man swung the seat left and right as he sat in it. For the moment he ignored the two boys who continued to stand resolutely in place. Except for boys gathering for roll call in the outer assembly area, there was a heavy stillness in the room where a heavy antiseptic smell seemed to come from a medicine cabinet hanging conspicuously on the wall. Behind and to the right of the Coach a wall was filled with framed pictures of school football and basketball teams. Trophies lined another shelf.

Coach Johnson crossed his leg and in one motion swiveled the chair so he faced the two boys. His eyes focused unflinchingly upon the youths and then stern blue eyes looked them up and down. "Something happened between you two and I want to know what it was." He waited expectantly when Peter and Ralph exchanged confused glances at one another.

Peter shifted his weight from one foot to the other. He took a quick look at Ralph, hoping his friend would answer, but the boy only shoved his tongue into his cheek forcing a large lump in his jowl - he said nothing. Drummed fingers on the desk was a warning that the adult was losing his patience.

Johnson pulled open the top drawer of his desk and took out a demerit pad. He flipped the pages, it was the only sound in the room. We're going to stay here all night until you tell me what happened." Peter gazed at the floor, there was still no response. The Coach started writing in the degrading book. He gave the boys a serious look and advised, "You know what happens if I give you both demerits?" He knew if he really pressed the issue he could reach Peter for an answer.

The youngster's bottom lip protruded. He flashed another quick look at the impassive Ralph, it was to no avail. Peter eyed the damnable book which meant he would lose all his free time. He would have to do extra chores and then this meant losing vacation days as well. Finally, he would be ridiculed by the other students at meal time when he could not have any deserts.

The boy blurted, "Sir, Ralph and me was playing in the hay loft." His lips tightened into a guilty half smile when he confessed, "We was playing without permission, Sir." He had not other choice than to try and fall on the Coach's mercy. But the burly man knew the real story had not come out. "Is that all you were doing?" he asked skeptically.

"Well," the boy hesitated, "Ralph...." He looked down ashamedly, then blurted, "Ralph fell, Sir. He fell from the loft to the barn floor, Sir." The boy blinked nervously trying to avoid Coach's gaze. Tears slipped down his cheeks. "Sir, Ralph got hurt real bad."

Suddenly, Ralph's elbow poked into the ribs of his friend. He gave the boy a stony glare. Peter took a step away and shouted, "I've got to tell him, Ralph. You mighta busted your ribs. You coulda killed yourself. You was unconscious and you scared me." Each boy's eyes were fixed on each other until Peter buried his face into his hands now weeping uncontrollably.

Coach chewed the end of his pencil. He ordered Benson to remove his shirt. The boy resisted the command. Coach set his jaw determinedly. "Face the door, Benson." The Instructors voice was strained and demanding. Finally, Ralph did as he was ordered. Johnson pressed his fingers into the belligerent boy's side. A piercing, pain-filled scream filled the room. Benson collapsed to the floor now gasping for breath.

Peter looked in horror. He dropped to his knees and he crawled to his fallen friend. "Ralph! Ralph!" he pleaded through sobs. The youngster was ordered out of the room while Coach took care of the emergency. Distraught and afraid Peter pressed his ear against the closed door when he heard Coach Johnson on the phone ordering the boat be made ready for a boy with possible internal injuries. Suddenly, the assembly room filled with boys waiting for roll call. Catcalls and rough housing filled the large room. Donlevy blew a shrill whistle and order was instantly restored. Peter, red faced and numbed by what happened in the cubicle stepped to his position and silently toed the line.

Donelevy's voice reached out to the subdued group, "Report." He ordered. He looked to his left and down the line of new Johnnies. A young voice spoke out strongly, "Benson's missing, Sir." Peter felt a shiver rush down his spine. He took a deep breath and exhaled slowly when he volunteered that Ralph was on his way to the hospital.

CHAPTER FOUR

THE RESTING PLACE

It was the next day when the New Johnnies gathered at the lower end of the football field. At their left twelve miniature wooden cottages flanked a cindered oval track. Peter Pappas had seen the quaint small shacks from the base of the flag pole which dominated the highest point on the island. The flag pole was now sandwiched between two of the incomplete dormitories.

He often wondered about the mysterious structures with miniature porches and tiled roofs that defended against storms blasting in from the North. But, at the time everything was too new. It did not matter that they existed at all.

At the front of the group Mister Clifton pointed to the first of the miniature cottages where a sign read, "City Hall." Peter viewed the cottages while listening intently as the Instructor explained the concept of what was known as Cottage Row and the Cottage Row Government. It was first thought of in 1888 when students were given bed ticking which they fashioned into tents. Later the boys gave up living in the exposed tents. Clifton then asked, "Why would they give up living in their tents? Who can give an answer?"

At first there was an uncomfortable stir between the students until on finally answered, "Fleas, Sir."

Clifton smiled reassuringly, "Good answer, but not the right one. Okay, who's next?"

"Skeeters, Sir." Another answered amid giggles of approval from the boys. "Nor'Easters?" The chatter continued approvingly.

"Not right yet, boys. Let's keep going." Clifton kept pressing for the correct answer.

"The cold, sir?" Peter's voice rose above the buzz of excitement from the others.

Clifton's gaze froze for a moment when he bellowed, "You're right!" Peter broke into a nervous grin. He hated it when he proved the other students wrong. In grammar school his penchant for detail - of isolating fragments missed by the others stuck in his mind and too often looked too much the smarty pants.

Clifton continued the lesson when he explained that three years earlier, in 1891, the Headmaster decided to let the boys build a single cottage which was quickly followed by another. More were added until there were twelve in all. The Instructor swept his arm in the direction of the twelve and explained that one called 'City Hall' was so named because the whole concept was that of a miniature government with an elected mayor. Buying student shares gave voting rights. He assured the boys that they too would be a part of this government.

Peter was glad when the tour ended. He could not concentrate. His mind was focused on Ralph. The tour was a distraction to him where he quickly became inattentive and moody. He had trouble sleeping the night before when he kept blaming himself for the terrible fall that injured his best friend.

Later, when breakfast was finished, Headmaster Williamson stood in place at the corner table. It was a signal he had an announcement before dismissing the students. A hush fell heavily when the administrator began solemnly, "Last evening a student by the name of Ralph Benson had an accident in the barn and as a result he received serious internal injuries..

Peter gripped the edge of his seat tightly. The portly Headmaster continued, "I'm sorry to announce that Ralph Benson died as a result of those injuries. Gasps filled the dining room. Peter sat in shock. He clasped his hands to his face, focusing unflinchingly at the corner table. His face drained when he felt a sudden urge to faint. Tears cascaded in a flood and here the boy buried his face into his trembling hands when the room seemed to spin out of control.

Suddenly, with breath filled sobs his stricken voice rose shrilly, "NO! NO!" he shouted, "HE'S NOT DEAD!" His eyes brimming with tears he buried his face into his hands heaving uncontrollable sobs. In moments unknown hands comforted the boy who was led out of the dining room. Curious stares from the other students followed the distraught Peter.

The Headmaster went on to explain, "Since Benson is an orphan we have been asked to bury him in our own cemetery here on the island." He looked over the sea of somber faces and said with finality, "You will all attend this service."

Later, that night, Peter, sat alone on the bench under the old elm tree. His thoughts recounted Ralph's curses - so spontaneous and carefree. He then wrapped his arms across his chest while staring off in space, he whished Ralph was there to hug him if only to chase away his feelings of hopelessness. All his hopes wilted. Rain began falling only to be ignored sad little boy.

Thunder and lightning snapped more violently that night. The wind rustled leaves high on the ponderous elm, but it did not matter to Peter for his thoughts were so enwrapped in his vigil. His heart beat raced rapidly when he recounted how he leaped at poor Ralph which caused him to lose his balance and crash to the barn floor. Gritting his teeth he looked up at the gray sky where raindrops mixed with his salty tears.

From the assembly room a man's voice yelled above the noise of the raging storm. But, the boy failed to hear him. "Pappas! Get in here !" the voice demanded. Finally, Peter slowly entered the vacant assembly room. A deep look of concern was etched behind Clifton's wire-framed glasses. "What in God's name were you doing out there?" he asked. Peter simply hunched his shoulders instead of answering.

Suddenly a hand gripped the boy's arm and twisted him around where he faced Couch Johnson who was kneeling before him. "And how's young Pappas doing? He asked with a twinkle in his eye.

"Wet!" Clifton answered sarcastically, "Seems he got caught in a storm."

"Well, I've got a job for him in a few minutes." The Coach winked at Clifton, "Come to the cubicle, Peter." He placed his large hand on the boy's shoulder and led him inside.

In the cubicle the Coach tossed the boy a football jersey and made him change out of his wet shirt. He then pointed to a tall stool where the youngster immediately clamped his feet around the rungs. The swivel chair creaked noisily when the burly man sat into it. Finally, he asked, "You and Benson were real good friends, weren't you?" The boy simply nodded. His eyes drifted to where Ralph had stood before he....before he.... The thought lingered.

Peter felt awkward alone with the Coach. The man was known for being tough, although very fair with the students. In some small way the Instructor reminded him of his own father, for his Dad was also surrounded with a family of five boys at various stages of rebelliousness. Dad was tough, otherwise he could never have gotten through all those terrible tragedies that marked his life. He was fair, never taking sides in teenage arguments, but acted more the mediator than the disciplinarian.

"You like being called Petee?" the Coach tried to put the solemn youth at ease. "Yes, Sir." The boy's voice was weak, yet responsive. Warm, attentive eyes were fixed on the boy. The Coach rubbed his lower lip pensively for he wanted to pull the youngster out of his depression.

"Most of the kids call you Pappas, don't they?" "Yes Sir." He answered while his eyes followed a fly flitting around the single light near the ceiling. He wanted to be left alone. He wanted to cry for Ralph, but would anyone understand? He learned that lesson when his Mom died. He was nine years old. His brother Chris took him aside during the wake and said, "We'll never see her again, Petee." He remembered bursting into bubbling sobs when he pulled away and turned his back on his brother. Chris held him close. He explained how strong he had to be so he could help Yia Yia and his twin sister through this terrible time. It was then he knew tears made nothing better.

A creaky squeak came from the burly man's chair when he crossed his leg and searched his mind to find some way to break into the grief of the student. From outside the winds howled, bending weathered trees almost to the breaking point. Rain lashed the building and windows steamed when the cold water struck the panes.

Suddenly, an urgent knock on the door brought an alarm. The school boat Pilgrim Three had a broken bow line and was dangerously close to the breakwater - a breakwater made up of huge pilings to calm heaving ocean waves during storms such as these. The Coach slipped into his foul weather gear then looked at the young boy sitting on the stool. "Common, Petee." he ordered when he tossed a poncho to the lad, "I need your help."

Peter looked aghast. He struggled with the weighty slicker, "You.... You really need me, sir?" he asked incredulously. They raced out the door into torrential rains that swept the Island. Trees howled eerily where the driving winds blew into them. Peter followed the burly Coach who was already struggling for balance against gale-force winds. The one hundred ten pound boy leaned into the storm which was battering the weathered barn at his left. Cascading water flooded driveway gutters that surged and overflowed the cisterns at the base of the hill.

They raced the length of the long pier where mounting waves surged against the pilings holding up the wharf. The youngster's heart beat thunderously when he tried to keep up with the Coach. The wharf shuddered beneath his feet creating visions that the jetty could collapse into the raging sea. He wanted to run back to safety, but this was the first time anyone asked for his help and he was not about to let them down.

Finally, they reached the landing where the Pilgrim Three strained the only four inch rope-line secured on the stern. Older boys waited their orders when the Coach studied the problem. The bow of the steamer catapulted up and down from wave after crashing wave lifted the boat like a match stick. The breakwater loomed dangerously close.

"We need someone to board her." Coach Johnson shouted above the wailing wind.

Peter stood to one side. His fingers desperately gripped the handrail on the gangway when it too groaned under the stress of the pitching landing slip. He gaped in alarm when mounting waves surged massively into the breakwater, then continued their momentum until they exploded on the shore like an obsessed demon.

The boy tugged at the drawstring of his hood. Rain lashed his face. He wondered if anyone would help him if he fell into the raging sea. How could they, he reasoned, in one split second he could drown. Even if he knew how to swim it would be hopeless. He swallowed deeply. A tremor of fear raced through him.

A husky teen jumped onto the rear deck of the rolling Pilgrim, then he made his way to the pitching bow and flung a line to those on the dock. The Coach tied another thick four inch thick line to the end of the smaller line. The husky teen hauled it on board and secured it to a cleat on the bow. Coach signaled Petee to come his way and help him. He kept his eye on the frightened youth who edged his way cautiously past the gangway.

The big man wrapped his arms around the boy's frail shoulders and pulled him close to his own body. Coach Johnson and Petee both pulled on the line where the wind swept rain battered their faces. With the help of other boys the bow of the Pilgrim was slowly pulled closer. Peter suddenly fantasized he was Superman, hauling the boat all by himself. They would all be proud of him, even Ralph.... even Ralph.... His hood slipped off his head and the full force of the stinging rain washed his face.

Finally, the Pilgrim was docked and secured by another four inch line. The Coach looked at the scrawny twelve year old standing next to the strapping boat crew. He slung his arm around the youngster's shoulders when struggling back up the hill, "Great job, Petee." he praised the grinning boy who was so proud of his accomplishment.

It was the next day. The storm of the previous night had passed and the sun shone brightly, like an omen, for today Ralph Benson was to be buried. Peter quietly toyed with his cereal, shoving his spoon idly into his Cheerios and pushing them from side to side in the bowl. He felt numb. It was so much like the time his mother was waked. He had never seen a dead person before, although when he and his friends played in the field near the tenement they often found dead cats, but today, this was different.

In the funeral home his brother Chris lifted him so he could see his mother. He eyed the caked powders on her face. Rouge seemed so out of place because he was told Mom never wore make-up. He stared at her for a long silent moment, now fascinated that death was so final.

In that brief moment he felt nauseous from the smell of the flowers, but he brushed it aside. He never really knew Ma-Ma since she was taken away when he and Anna were still infants. Except for being with her briefly on that farm he finally accepted that now, nine years later, she came home. Now he knew where "that place" was that Yia-Yia kept such a secret. In "that place" Ma-Ma died alone and so far away from all of us.

He was startled when a gentle hand settled on his shoulder. Peter failed to hear the signal releasing the boys from breakfast. He also failed to hear the announcement that the student body would gather by the old elm tree for the long walk to the south end of the island where the miniature cemetery was located. He sat alone amongst the many empty tables, although a gentle hand still rested on his shoulder.

A woman's soft voice spoke from his left, "It's time to find a resting place for your friend Ralph." The voice spoke in a whisper. He swallowed deeply when his eyes flicked to a chair and when he looked up his blank, glistening eyes met those of Miss Pederson. She lowered her dark eye lashes for a moment and then smiled compassionately while reading his face meditatively. Suddenly, Peter burst into tears when he found himself enveloped in Miss Pederson's arms. "Ralph Benson was a lucky boy to have you as his friend." she whispered when she dabbed his tears with a tissue.

The procession stepped away from the old elm tree and descended the sloping hill, then followed the road which led to the south end. From somewhere near the barn a cow filled the air with an eerie lowing and then suddenly stopped. The sun shone brightly since the storm of the previous night when the Autumn day turned calm and chilly.

Peter with Miss Pederson holding his hand trailed the main body of students when the boy suddenly stopped. He faced the campus where he could barely make out the flag flying at half staff. Resting his eyes on the Bulfinch building he warmed up a thin smile.

"What are you thinking, Peter?" Pederson asked. The twelve year old nervously shuffled his feet as he gazed at some wistful yet distant memory. I remember when Ralph stood here and called me crazy 'cause of something I said." He hesitated, then continued, "I always said dumb things and Ralph....Ralph used to swear at me." He smiled shyly, "That was the day we came to see the peanut lady."

The adult took the young boy's hand and continued on. "I remember that day, Petee." She smiled down warmly at him, "You were the boy who stood away from the crowd. You kept staring at me as if there was question in your mind."

A flattered smile appeared on Peter's face, "You saw me?" He asked in surprise.

She squeezed his hand and answered, "I don't miss much. I was talking to Mister Clifton and from the corner of my eye I saw this boy watching me very queerly. That boy looked like he wanted something answered."

Peter smiled thinly when he remembered the event. "Yea, Ralph thought I was crazy cuz I thought you was a witch." He dared not look at her when his eyes widened at his gaff and then focused back at the Bulfinch building.

She chuckled at his innocence and asked, "Do you still think I'm a witch?"

Peter swallowed a lump in his throat. A blush flushed his cheeks. He answered sheepishly, "Naa. You're too nice to be a witch." He shrugged his shoulders and said, "I guess Ralph was right. I'm kinda stupid sometimes."

Their conversation dropped off suddenly. A few yards ahead the main body of students had entered a grove of trees. Peter knew they were close to the cemetery. A shiver rushed through him.

He hesitated, then looked at the white farm house to his left. "Aren't you afraid to live there alone?" he asked innocently. She did not answer him for she knew the boy was really trying to avoid the ordeal ahead. "I wouldn't want to be alone like you, Miss Pederson." His brow knit into a frown when he glanced out of the corner of his eyes and saw the entire student body assembling at the graveyard.

The botanist urged the hesitating boy along. Finally they arrived at the cemetery. A white picket fence enclosed the miniature grave site where it was blanketed entirely by Lilies-Of-The-Valley that spread their dainty white flowers throughout the burial plot. The striking, fragrant, bell shaped blooms lent a blend of tranquility to the austere setting.

The assembled students stood, by their class size outside the gate. At their left the school band solemnly played the hymn Rock-Of-Ages, somberly sending the soft tones reaching into the tall trees. Peter felt a chill rush through him. His hands felt clammy when he wiped them along his pant leg. He tried with all his might to hold back the tears he felt swelling inside him, but he knew all too well his feelings of grief could not be held back. He dared not look into the graveyard, but soon his eyes drifted to the open grave where Ralph Benson's bronzed casket lay suspended on straps over the grave site. The boy squeezed his eyes shut and bowed his head letting tears trickle down his cheeks.

From somewhere the youth heard a minister praying with the assemblage of students joining in reading psalms. But the twelve year old could only picture Ralph tumbling out of the hay loft and crashing helplessly on the wooden floor. He shoved his hands to his face when Miss Pederson knelt in front of him and pressed the trembling youngster into her arms.

The minister's voice possessed the moment when he concluded: "Ashes to ashes - Dust to dust And thus, Dear Jesus, we send unto thee the soul of Ralph Benson to rest with you in eternity."

The lonely notes of taps echoed through the grove when Peter suddenly turned away, his face a mask of grief and now agonized sobs were muffled when another hymn was played by the band. The botanist led Peter away, now guiding the troubled youth in the direction of the farm house. When they arrived the youngster sat quietly on a porch step. Dry, red rimmed eyes stared peacefully at a Robin jabbing the ground for earth worms. A glass of soda was suddenly placed into his hands. He looked into her eyes and gave her a shy, uncertain smile to thank her. For a moment not a word was spoken when she sat next to him, letting the sounds of Autumn enter their world.

Peter wanted her to hug him again like she did at the cemetery. He wanted her to draw him into her arms and stroke his head like his Yia Yia used to do when he was sad. He felt so uncomfortable with his thoughts because he knew the Instructors were under strict rules about getting too close to students. Suddenly, a man's voice interrupted his fantasy. "How's Petee holding up, Miss Pederson? Coach Johnson sat on the other side of the boy and nudged him playfully. She looked relieved that he had come and answered, "I think we've turned the corner, Coach. Peter's going to be a survivor." The boy smiled shyly, embarrassed at having shown so much emotion at the grave site. Didn't his brother Lou say, "Go out there and be a king." He gripped the edge of the bench with his two hands and slowly shook his head back and forth. "Yea, be a king."

CHAPTER FIVE

BIX AND ISAIAH

Classes had begun in September of 1942 when Peter entered the seventh grade. He was no longer a New Johnnie. He liked the idea that a new group of boys took up the apprenticeship. Finally, everyone was calling him Petee. But, there was still a nagging loneliness left by Ralph Benson's death, although Isaiah Feldman, another seventh grader and he were becoming real good friends.

They sat in a small waiting room which was directly beneath the dining room in Bowditch House. It was here all students reported to be called to meals. "How did you get a name like Isaiah?" Peter asked his classmate. His friend shrugged his shoulders when he answered , "It's in the bible. You know how fathers are, Petee. My father was a Rabbi and he named all of us kids from the Old Testament in the bible. My oldest brother's name is Mica and my sister is called Rachel." The boy felt uncomfortable talking about his heritage. He shrugged his shoulders and said, "I've been stuck with Isaiah, that's all."

He looked at Peter over wire framed glass which kept sliding down his nose until he shoved them back to his bridge where they belonged. Isaiah sat on the bench while staring at the floor meditatively. He was as thin as Peter and just about the same height, only Petee noticed the difference in height was directly the result of his friend slouching. Isaiah looked like the perfect studious type, a persona he hated and all of this came about because he liked to read books.

Peter chuckled at Isaiah's remark about being stuck with his name. "Yea, Isaiah, but you can't even make a nickname out of it. His friend drew a long breath, then released it slowly. He eyed his naive friend with a sideward glance and answered, "Some guys call me 'kike' and others call me 'god-damned-jew'." He smiled contemptuously. His forehead suddenly filled with an uneasy frown. "I hate nicknames, Petee." He gave his young friend a quick, caustic look and continued, "I hate nicknames." he repeated., "Petee, don't ever call me by one or the whole school will pick up on it and who knows what else they'll come up with."

Peter leveled a sympathetic look at the boy who now sat hunched over while looking at his shoes which dangled just off the floor. "I promise you, Isaiah, I'll never give you a nickname." He tried to make his voice icy firm. "It ain't nice to call people names." Peter became mockingly combative, "If I hear anyone call you bad names -I'm gonna hit 'em with all my might."

Feldman snickered at the remark, "Yea and then you'll end up with a busted nose." The boy smiled at Peter and then said with finality, "Hey, ya can't change it. It's always there and there ain't nothing you can do about it." A quick smile pinched his lips when he continued, "My father used to tell me that."

Mister Clifton suddenly appeared at the door which led to the dining room, "'Okay boys." he announced, "Birthday table boys go in first." Pappas and Feldman gathered next to the Instructor and were joined by four others. "You're the lucky ones today, guys. You're getting ice-cream cake for desert."

Seated at Headmaster Williamson's table the six boys who's birthdays fell in the month of September chatted idly, answering questions put to them by the trim and pretty Headmaster's wife. The boy's felt a mixed pride in their unaccustomed role as central figures now separated from the rest of the student body because of their birth dates. Polished silverware glittered under bright ceiling lights. Every napkin was folded in the shape of a fan. At each place setting a small gift was wrapped and awaited each boy.

Trying to use his best manners Peter slowly unfolded the fan-shaped napkin and placed it on his lap. Sitting across from him a young girl sat strangely quiet. She sat primly next to her mother, the Headmaster's wife, and seemed to be following a sophisticated regimen, so obviously correct.

It made Peter feel uncomfortable, however, since he lacked the knowledge of precise table manners he copied the young girl's movements - he knew he would be safe. She looked up when her mother whispered to her. Soft brown eyes inadvertently focused on Peter. A thin-lipped smile met his gaze and then she abruptly stared at her empty plate. Long brown eye lashes looked frozen in place.

Peter was fascinated. His eyes flit from the Headmaster's wife and then back to the girl, for he found such an uncanny resemblance of the two. Long straight brown hair draped over the girl's shoulders and disappeared somewhere down her back, while a simple yellow bow was fixed just above her forehead.

Mrs. Williamson noticing the awkward lack of introduction immediately said, "This is our daughter Sheryl-Ann who has recently completed her early years at a private girl's school." The adult named all the boys for her daughter and continued, "Sheryl-Ann will be attending classes on the island, starting in the seventh grade until she reaches high school and then she'll be off to another private girl's school.

With the school prayer over the meal was served. Peter found his courage and spoke to the shy Sheryl-Ann. "They call me Petee." he flashed a simple smile at the girl.

"She returned a patronizing smile and answered softly, "They call me Sherry or Ann."

Peter's courage had now built immensely when he continued, "I hear you're gonna be in my class this year." His eyebrows rose expectantly. Feldman's knee tapped Peter's leg and interrupted, "She's going to be in our class." Isaiah emphasized the "our" and sat back satisfied with himself. Peter was annoyed with his friend since he was trying to make a good impression on the girl. He finally said, "Oh, this is Isaiah. He's in our class too."

The gift which sat to the right of his dinner plate caught the boy's eye. He was uncomfortable trying to keep a conversation interesting with Sheryl-Ann and thought it was the right moment to cut the small talk. He tugged at the string which wrapped his gift. Finally, he opened the box. He held up a glass domed paperweight which he turned upside down to let imitation snow float onto a miniature farm which was glued to the foundation. His eyes sparkled in delight.

He failed to hear the Headmaster ask him his age for the boy was still absorbed with the dazzling snow falling inside the paperweight. Williamson repeated the boys name and waited. Peter looked up quickly, still not realizing he had been asked a question. He bubbled with enthusiasm when he said, "I love my gift, Sir."

Williamson pursed his lips. Round brown eyes flashed behind thick glasses. The young boy realized he missed something, then quickly apologized. He looked at the other students hoping they would clue him, but they only stared back unsympathetically. Sheryl-Ann simply smiled at his predicament. Feldman nudged him with his knee again and whispered, "He wants to know how old you are."

Alarmed at his indiscretion, he blurted, "I'm twelve....I mean.... I mean...." He stammered, "I'm thirteen, Sir." A sudden blush filled his cheeks when the corners of his mouth lifted into a half smile. Mrs. Williamson came to the boy's defense. She cast a condescending smile at the unnerved youngster and asked, "Why do you like your gift so much, Peter?"

Pappas smiled nervously, "I like it cuz it's snowing. I love the snow, Ma-am." He glanced at Sheryl-Ann, then turned away thinking his answer was stupid.

The Headmaster then asked, "Have you ever worked outside on a snowy day, young man?"

An open youthful face answered, "No Sir, but I sure would like to." He shuffled his feet nervously under the table and accidentally kicked Sheryl-Ann. Their eyes suddenly fixed on one another. The boy looked in shock. His mouth dropped open, then he mutely mouthed an apology.

Feldman suppressed a snicker at the awkward situation his friend placed himself. But the serious Headmaster did not let the incident pass when he eyed both boys critically. He gave his daughter a quick disapproving frown and then focused his attention on the two boys. "Is there something funny in what I asked Pappas, Feldman?" Isaiah shrank back into his chair, blinking anxiously he meekly answered, "No Sir." He removed his glasses and timidly wiped them with his napkin.

"Where do you and Feldman work your four hour shifts?" The superior's penetrating gaze was fixed on Peter's unblinking eyes. The boy gulped, then answered softly, "Me and Feldman work in the Thomas dormitory, Sir."

The next question was quick and decisive, "Do you like working in the dormitory?" For a moment Pappas did not know how to answer him, but he knew his answer better be a positive one. He was hesitant with his answer and then spoke hastily, "We clean the halls and stairs. We wash the bathrooms and stuff like that." He sucked in his breath when he glanced at Feldman who was sitting rigidly in his chair.

The Headmaster sat back, dabbing his lips with his napkin. A cynical smile signaled he was enjoying the banter with the student. Finally, he spoke cuttingly, "Now that's not the kind of work a thirteen year old should be doing, is it?" His sarcasm swept the table. Peter felt overwhelmed with all the attention focused on him. "Sir," he answered, "I'd rather be doing work like the big guys." He bit his lower lip nervously when his eyes drifted to Sheryl-Ann who had a fixed stony look at her father. Mrs. Wiliamson simply smiled at the badgering.

The administrator grinned broadly. Leaning forward he spoke slowly, 'Tomorrow morning, at five o'clock, you and Feldman will report to Mister Armbrewster at the new barn." Peter's face drained. Feldman gasped and sat back wide-eyed and confused. Peter then blurted in surprise, "B....Before breakfast, Sir?"

There was no humor in the Headmaster's voice when he looked over the tops of his glasses and answered, "Of course, young man, farmers keep very early hours. Cows have to be milked and fed. Pigs have to be slopped. Horses must be groomed, eggs have to be gathered. And don't forget manure, must be cleaned up.

He seemed to be enjoying the position he had placed the boys, "Don't forget," he continued, "this Spring fields have to be planted, weeded and then," he winked at his wife, "remember, we have fifty acres that must be cultivated." A heavy silence fell over the table when Mister Williamson said with finality, "Since you have to be up by four in the morning it means you'll have to get to bed by at least seven o'clock. Doesn't it?" His eyebrows rose where a warm smile ended the conversation.

Peter cast a quick look at Feldman who sat stunned by the discourse. Thirteen year old Peter broke into a nervous grin when he simply agreed, "Yes Sir. Before breakfast, Sir." He sat back into his chair, now mulling over the terrible ordeal he had paced himself and his friend. His eyes drifted to Sheryl-Ann who looked at him sympathetically. He smiled shyly for he recognized that she disapproved of the position her father placed him.

When the boys were dismissed Feldman's anger flared, "What a birthday present you got for us. You made eyes at his daughter, Petee. He saw you. And ....And look what you did with your big mouth." Peter looked bewildered. His thoughts were in a scramble. He knew Isaiah was right, but he did not think he did anything to provoke the Headmaster. "I....I don't know what I did wrong, Isaiah."

"You want to be like the big guys. That's what you told him. And he saw you making goo-goo eyes at his daughter. Jeez, Petee, we're gonna freeze our butts off working on the farm."

It was early the next morning when Mark Armbewster stood alone in front of the massive doors which opened into the cavernous white barn. A September chill mixed with morning dew formed a ghost-like fog that hung eerily in the lowlands. Ambrewster shifted his Panama hat from his brow to the back of his head. Sunglasses were an unused timeless feature that fit snugly on his brow. Bushy eyebrows were showing tinges of gray which matched graying sideburns. After a lifetime of working outdoors his skin was tough and leathery.

He was the Chief Administrator of the farm and he had leaned long ago to be strict with teenage boys who were often irresponsible. The boys roughhoused too much and all too often this led to injuries. Fifteen years of working with teens forced him to change his ways from an easy going guy to a disciplinarian. He hated it.

He purposely waited at the entrance to the barn for he had been told that two boys were to start work on the farm that morning. They were already late.

Hurried footsteps raced down the graveled walk and then stopped just to the side of the barn. Two young boys waited breathlessly until the Instructor turned and faced them. Peter gulped nervously. The head farmer studied the frail youths who were told to report that morning. He looked at his watch and said, "You were told to be here at five, not five-thirty." It was an awkward moment for the boys did not know what to say.

Peter took a sideward glance into the barn where his eyes settled on the place where Ralph had his accident. He squeezed his eyes tightly at the memory. Finally, dismissing the thought he faced Armbrewster and said, "I'm Petee Pappas, Sir."

At Armbrewster's command they followed him to the other end of the barn which blazed with lights. Before they entered the head farmer pointed to a small loading dock with a five foot by five foot hole directly in the center. He told the boys to remember the dock for it would be a big part of the job he planned for them.

Finally, they entered the brightly lit cow barn and were overwhelmed by a strong stench of sweating cowhide. Fifty head of beefy Guernsey cows stood in two neat rows. Each animal was secured in place by a clamp devise around its neck so it would not roam.

Throughout the cow barn teenaged milking crews huddled next to their cows - manipulating fingers expertly extracted milk from the udders. Galvanized pails clamped between the knees of a boy-milkers quickly filled with the creamy liquid. Armbrewster led the way, explaining that each cow had a name and the sign over its head indicated which bull was the sire.

Peter looked confused when he innocently asked, "What's sire mean, Sir?"

The adult smiled at him and said, "Son, that's who the cow's father is."

"They have father's?" the teen asked in surprise. From next to a cow being milked a voice blurted, "Oh my gawd." To the surpise of the milker his cow shifted her position, raised its rear leg and kicked forward. The hoof caught the milker's pail, dumping the liquid contents into the manure gutter behind the cow. In that instant the cow, now frantic from the noisy pail, drove her flank into the surpised youth, tossing him to the ground where he lay sprawled in the manure filled and sodden milk.

Both Peter and Isaiah screeched with laughter, then instantly muffled themselves when Armbrewster raged at the incompetence of the milker. The young milker shot a sour look at the boys who dared laugh at him. It was not wise to anger an older boy.

They arrived at a storage room in the back of the barn. From behind, the pulsating sound of milk meeting tin pails sounded rhythmic. Squish - squish - squish/squish/squish and then again, squish - squish/squish/squish. The two inexperienced boys were told to each take a long handle shovel and a wheelbarrow and follow the Instructor. It was an awkward attempt by the boys to try and maneuver the unfamiliar wheelbarrows, for the cumbersome tool pitched left and right on its single steel wheel. Peter and Isaiah grimly tried with all their might to steer the unwieldy contraption in a straight line, however, no matter how hard they tried it turned out to be a clumsy ordeal.

Back in the main barn Mister Armbrewster explained, "You've seen the front of the cows, boys," a measured smile appeared on the adult's face when he continued, "This is the other end." He pointed at a long line of flailing tails. Behind all the cows a cement trench stretched endlessly to the front of the barn. The two boys turned up their noses at the trench with its manure filled to capacity. Quick looks of foreboding flashed between the two youngsters.

The head farmer explained, "Pappas, you start here. You'll use your shovel to clean out the manure and dump each shovel full into your wheelbarrow. When you've filled the barrow," he continued, "you'll push it to that outside platform I pointed out to you earlier and dump the manure into the hole." He then instructed Feldman to do the same thing in the second row." With all of that said he walked away leaving the two boys with their mouths hanging open in disbelief.

The boys fixed their eyes on the yawning gutter. Peter chuckled at the absurdity of the job ahead and Feldman, following Peter's lead, burst into a nervous giggle. Now caught up in their released emotions the two boys leaned on their shovels and erupted in laughter. Petee pointed at the huge row of cow-dung and held his nose sputtering "It's....It's cow poop-dee-doo!" Isaiah clapped his hands to his face and answered in disgust, "Yea, and look, we've go to clean it up"

The boy's mockingly cried and then in one pulse of hysteria Peter shouted, "How in hell are we going to eat breakfast after shoveling this crap?"

It was moments later when the scraping shovels filled with its smelly contents found their way into the wheelbarrows. Peter labored grimly for the dung was now weighted with urine. Each shovel full seemed heavier than the last. Taking a quick look at the other side he smiled to himself where he saw Feldman's head bobbing behind the line of rumps on that side. He wanted to tease his friend, but he noticed his own wheelbarrow was now filled to capacity and he became apprehensive if he could ever move it.

The puny boy gripped each handle then strained to lift it with one monumental heave. The overloaded barrow suddenly pitched to the right. Peter tried with all his might to keep the wheelbarrow from tipping - it was useless. In that bungling motion the damnable single wheeled conveyance drove into the gutter spilling the reeking content heaped behind an innocent cow's legs.

The frightened animal bellowed loudly when it lurched to the side. Peter stared helplessly at the foul, pungent mess he created.

His bottom lip wavered until he clamped it tightly with his top teeth. He desperately looked up the aisle for help when suddenly a milker shouted, "You stupid ass, Pappas. Don't fill it so full."

Suddenly, a rugged red headed youth scolded the bewildered boy. "Jeezus Cripes, Pappas what the hell's the matter with you?" Peter sucked in his breath and tried to explain, but the angry red head ignored him and with one hand righted the wheelbarrow. "You've stunk up this whole cow barn." he snapped. "We're gonna smell this shit for a week."

Peter looked terrified. His only thought was that Armbrewster would give him a demerit on his first day. The angry red head's frown soon disappeared. His anger quickly subsided. "Commere kid." he ordered. Peter hesitated. "I said commere so I can show you how to handle this thing.." He set the wheelbarrow on its rear legs and spoke more softly, "Get over here, pal." He tried to downplay his outburst. "How'n the hell do they expect you to learn when they don't show you how to do it?"

Peter jumped over the flooded mess and stood next to the burly older student. He lifted shovel full after shovel full of the smelly manure and dumped it into the wheelbarrow. When it was half filled he said, "Okay, now see if you can lift the barrow." The youngster hesitatingly gripped the handles where for some unexplained reason he found the courage to lift the cumbersome wheelbarrow then found it relatively easy to lift. He lit up into a bright smile when he cried out, "I did it! I did it!"

The older boy kept encouraging the struggling youth when the barrow began to move. Steel wheels easily clipped over the rough cement floor. As he gained more speed the supporting milker raced along side. Once through the door the challenging ramp loomed ahead. The wheelbarrow teetered precariously from left to right once the single wheel struck the wooden incline which creaked noisily with the burdensome load. The voice from behind kept urging the more confident Peter to aim the awkward carrier at the approaching hole in the center of the dock.

The closer he got the smaller the opening seemed to appear. Could he make it? Peter's doubts were rising instantly, however, he had no time to think of failure, not now when he was so close to success. Vibrations from the barrow were now making him skeptical.

The hole in the middle of the dock loomed like an open mine pit. The youngster aimed the barrow in its direction when suddenly he could not control the momentum. The handles were instantly wrenched out of his hands when the wheel pitched into the hole, scattering the manure onto the platform. The hulking wheelbarrow, too big to fit in the hole was sticking up perpendicularly, its handles projected upward like a pair of stiff legs.

The boy backed away from the new mess and swallowed with difficulty. The stillness of the early morning was now shattered where roosters from the nearby chicken coups led a cacophony of shrill frightened cock-a-doodle-doos. A calm voice from the older boy said, "I've never seen anything like this happen before." Peter's firm, anxious gaze met the sparkling, mischievous smile fixed on the red head's face.

The framed silhouette of head farmer Armbrewster stood at the entrance to the dairy barn. His hands were planted firmly on his hips when he asked, "You having a problem with that wheelbarrow, Pappas?" The Administrator's voice cut like a knife. The youngster's face paled when he turned abruptly and faced the Instructor. He tried to answer, but his voice failed him. A feeling of hopeless abandon filled every one of his senses.

"Bixby, did you allow this to happen?" Armbrewster shot pointed looks, first at the upturned wheelbarrow and then back to the surprised milker. Peter, realizing someone else was about to be blamed for his folly answered, "Sir, I....I," his voice trailed off to a whisper, "did it." He slowly took a step backward and away from the incriminating wheelbarrow.

The farmer snapped at the retreating boy, "I was speaking to Bixby, young feller." A stony glare filled the boy with fear.

The burly milker stepped behind the thirteen year old who was still retreating backward. He placed large hands on the boy's bony shoulders and held him firmly and then answered, "Sir, it was my fault. I should have been more careful." Bixby squeezed Peter's shoulders more tightly when the boy tried to wrench away in protest. "No....No....It was my fault." The youth objected.

Suddenly a finger stabbed the air, now pointing directly at the struggling boy. "I told you I was talking to Bixby." Large blue eyes gazed pleadingly at the angry Administrator, when suddenly they just looked helplessly at the man. "I should give you both a demerit for this." he snapped as he walked away.

Peter was dumbfounded. He wanted to shout to the adult, but he knew better than to open his mouth. Armbrewster disappeared around the corner of the barn. "Common, kid," the older boy's voice was calm and reassuring. He gripped the protruding handle and pointed at the other one for the youngster to grab. In one tug the wheelbarrow was back on the platform. "Don't worry about the demerit. Armbrewster's bark is worse than his bite." Bixby gave the boy a quick smile, "Most of the time he never puts in that demerit. He only uses it as a threat."

"But it was all my fault - not yours." The boy still had a problem tying to figure it out.

"Okay, kid, let's forget about it.." Bixby pushed the wheelbarrow to the door of the dairy barn and pointed for Peter to take over. He then asked, What do they call a little squirt like you?"

Peter gripped the two handles and pushed the barrow while smiling at his success at handling it. "They call me, Petee." he finally answered.

The older boy smiled modestly when he said, "I'm Bill Bixby. But, don't call me Bill." he warned, "Call me Bix or I won't answer you."

The youngster returned to his original position at the gutter. He looked over at Feldman who's wheelbarrow was fully loaded. "Better take some of that off." he volunteered professionally. A grunt came from his friend when he too began removing the heaped pile. "We'll never get this done at this rate." he complained.

Peter struggled successfully to clean a portion of the long stretched gutter that lay ahead of him. Suddenly, from behind a cow's tail lifted and droppings of manure plopped noisily into the trough. The boy looked back in disgust to where he had just cleaned the trench and helplessly questioned, "Jeez, why do they do that after I just cleaned it?" His question was quickly answered by a nearby milker, "Hey kiddo! Don't-cha know they gotta let it out so's we can get the milk?"

A puzzled expression appeared on Peter's face. He pushed another shovel full of manure into his wheelbarrow which brought him abreast of the milker who had just spoken. "You mean the cow has to poop before it can be milked?" Peter asked naively.

"Yea. You got the idea." The milker turned his face so as not to betray his joke.

"Is that why there's so much of it." The thirteen year old asked innocently.

"Well, it's like this, kid." The milker continued, "I'm milking a special cow. And what makes it special is that it's the only cow with a star on its teat." Nimble fingers extracted the milk from the teats, squirting streams of milk into half the filled bucket. "And because this cow has a star on its teat is cuz its manure is richer than the other cows." The boy peered out of the corner of his eyes at the inquiring boy; a mischievous smile crossed his lips. "Go ahead, smell it." He encouraged.

Peter stood in thought. He lifted a shovel full of the supposed richer manure and studied it. "You mean cuz this cow's got a star it makes it a better cow than the others?" the boy's eyes widened when he focused on the contents of the shovel.

"You got the idea, pal. Go ahead, smell it."

"And this manure is better than the rest?" the youngster eyed the contents skeptically when he brought the shovel closer to his nose. He took a deep smell, freezes for a second, then dropped the offending shovel back onto the wheelbarrow. "Yuk!" he blurted when he clamped his fingers to his nose, "It don't smell no different than the other poop." He protested.

His protagonist set his lips resolutely so he would not betray himself by laughing and giving his mischief away. "Yup," he finally answered through a faltering smile, "But it's not only the manure that makes the cow better, it's the star." He pointed at one of the four teats protruding from the cow's udder. Now grinning like a demonic gargoyle the milker pushed his stool back offering the simplistic boy an opportunity to look closer at the teat pointed at him.

"You've got to get closer than that, pal." The milker encouraged. Peter inched his way between the cow and the older boy and looked curiously at the udder. "Look just under my fingers and you'll see the star. Pappas shifted himself for a better look when suddenly a stream of milk splattered his face. Shocked by the unexpected deluge the youngster pitched backward where his right foot stepped solidly into the manure-filled gutter. Wrenching himself from his predicament his momentum tripped him onto the fully loaded wheelbarrow which tipped when the weight of his body struck it solidly.

The boy lay sprawled on the cement floor with a blanket of manure from the upturned wheelbarrow covering him. Finally, he recovered from his humiliation just enough to shoot a stony glare at his adversary, "You did that on purpose." He yelled hysterically. "Look what you did to me." The youngster's rage mounted helplessly. Laughter by the surrounding milkers filled the barn while the boy tried fruitlessly to clean the offensive debris off his clothes.

From behind Isaiah Feldman arrived to see what the commotion was about. He looked at his friend with a fixed scowl on his face. "Boy, do you stink, Petee." He blurted as he tried to suppress a snicker. Peter looked at his friend for help when he said, "Look what he did to me.." He pulled his shirt away from his body, a look of disgust filled his face. "Ike, what am I going to do?"

Isaiah looked horrified. Bulging eyes glared behind his glasses, "you called me 'IKE' Petee!" His voice rose hysterically when he exchanged confused glances at the gathering milkers. "Now they're all gonna call me 'IKE'!" Peter looked dumbfounded and suddenly he remembered Isaiah never wanted a nickname. He made it a point that Peter should never ever think of one for him. But, "IKE' simply popped out.

Isaiah's heart raced with his anger. He was incredulous his best friend would break a trust not to give him any kind of nickname. He squeezed his eyes shut as if to ward off any other reference by the rest of the boys clustered around the spillage. Petee looked aghast at his friend's emotional outburst and for the moment forgot about his own predicament.

He came closer to his distraught friend and said, "It's only a name, Feldman." But this explanation would not do when the troubled boy whispered, "Now they'll call me, "Ike the kike!" Don't you understand? He turned and abandoned his helpless friend.

Peter looked stunned when his friend turned on his heel and disappeared through the barn. He stood dumbfounded, confused with is thoughts in disarray when he questioned, "What did he mean by Kike?"

Suddenly, a voice spoke from behind. The thirteen year old turned to find Bix at his left. "It's okay, Petee." he calmed the boy by simply being there. "Lots of guys don't like nicknames. But in a school like this they're going to give you one anyway." Bix was a rugged boy with very clear eyes which seemed to offer comfort no matter what the turmoil. He looked sympathetically at his young charge and said, "You know, Petee. You stink." The youngster simply smiled shyly and hunched his shoulders in frustration.

A week later found Peter on his knees tugging carrots out of the ground for it was harvest time for vegetables. From his vantage point he could see Miss Pederson's farm house in the distance. "Jeez, my knees are killing me." His complaint was aimed at five other boys, each of whom was responsible for tending the carrots in other rows. "You ain't seen nothing' kiddo." the retort was cutting, "Wait 'till you start pulling those tough long root beets."

The thirteen year old sat back on his haunches while pressing his hands into his aching spine. "Beets?" he questioned. The others conspiratorially smiled at each other until one of them said, "Yea, beets attract all kinds of bugs too. A snicker passed between the other boys.

"Bugs? What kinda bugs? Peter disliked bugs for he lived with them in the tenement which often gave him the creeps. Cockroaches, flies and of all things those crawly bed-bugs. Of course we cannot forget the huge cellar water bugs that brought him misery. He started to ask another question when he frowned down at himself and decided not to.

One of the boys stopped working and faced the perspiring questioner, "Green, slimy ones with prickly things on their backs. And then there's the skeeters." The boy continued with his vile descriptions when Peter interrupted, "But we got skeeters here. I've been killing 'em. That's why I put my shirt back on.

The boy gave Peter a mischievous smile, "Not like these skeeters, Petee boy. These skeeters come cuz of the bugs." He wrinkled his face and grinned demonically, for he knew Peter was showing a shred of fear. "Those bugs are so big the skeeters come in and suck the blood right out of "em." Peter's eyes were unflinchingly focused on the story teller, "Then these big, enormous skeeters come after us cuz we're there to be eaten too."

Peter suddenly gave the boy a hard look when he countered, "I don't think skeeters are that big, Armstrong. How come we don't have 'em biting us right now? It's the same island and they all come from the same place, don't they?"

The antagonist pounced on the sudden negative in Peter's voice, "No they don't, Petee. These skeeters would get eaten by those big bugs. That's why the bigger skeeters come to suck the blood out of'em before they suck the blood out of us."

Peter turned away, "Ah, you're full of it, Armstrong." He stepped over the row of carrots he had been harvesting and started for the dirt road at the edge of the field. Suddenly, a shout from behind warned, "Ya got one of those green slimy bugs on your back, Pappas."

The thirteen year old swallowed a lump in his throat. He reluctantly stood rigidly in place. "Where is it, Armstrong." He asked through clenched teeth. He thought he could feel hundreds of crawling legs creeping on the back of his neck.

"It's on your shirt collar." Armstrong's voice was now more dramatic as Peter stretched his neck trying to see what was on his collar; he unwillingly gave up the search when it proved fruitless.

"It's trying to crawl onto your skin, Petee. Stand still and I'll sneak up on it and pull it off." Peter failed to hear the snickers coming from the other boys who had stopped all work while the drama unfolded. He heard Armstrong's footsteps approaching nearer and nearer when suddenly a well aimed slap at the nape of Peter's neck sprawled the victim into the dusty ground.

Bursts of laughter filled the acreage when the stunned thirteen year old twisted onto his back and angrily glared at the guffawing Armstrong who hovered over him. "I killed it, Pappas." He bragged as he pretended to wipe his hand down the side of his dungarees. The stunned Peter drew his hand across the back of his neck, then studied his palm for any sign of the carcass - nothing was there.

He realized he was the butt of a cruel joke, but it would be useless to even try to attack his adversary who was so much bigger than him. Peter squatted on a rock and slowly dusted off his pants. His mind was in a turmoil, for her remembered how he was made a fool I in the cow barn and now this new episode would surely bring chuckles to the many boys in such a close knit society. Peter started to speak, frowns down at himself and decides it would be better to let the matter drop.

"Better get back to work, Pappas." Armstrong spoke over his shoulder when he trudged to the row of carrots he was picking.

The other boys also returned to their labors with an occasional look at the seated scapegoat and then completely ignored him. Peter walked away toward the dirt road. From high in the trees the raucous chatter of crows filled the air. The boy took a quick look at them then spoke in a whisper, "Go ahead, you damn birds. Laugh at me like those guys did. But, I'll show you. Some day I'm gonna get that Armstrong. And he's gonna beg me for mercy. He'll see." He doubled his fist and swung at an imaginary opponent.

In the distance the boys working the carrot patch watched the lad walk away. Their voices filled the air with warnings that Armbrewster would surely issue a demerit for walking off without permission. But, Peter's thoughts were mixed. At first he thought he should stop and see Miss Pederson at the old farm house. She understood him better than anyone else and....he liked her.

He jammed his hands into his pockets and with his head held low he eyed stones along the dirt road and kicked them aimlessly. He knew he was in trouble for leaving his assignment without permission. He also knew that no student was allowed to roam the island without a special okay. It was a rule drilled into every student's mind.

Suddenly, three low flying combat airplanes appeared from the mainland. Crooked, gull-like wings held four menacing machine guns, two under each wing. A few feet from the wingtips silver bombs were cradled like oversized eggs. Peter instinctively waved at the flying machines. He shouted loudly, but the drone of the planes engines muffled his attempt to be recognized and the hope the pilots would dip their wings at him. "Common Corsair's! Common fighters!"

Go get those subs." A disappointed expression filled his eyes when the planes passed directly over him without a dip of the wings. They quickly flew off in the direction of the north end of the island and out to sea.

When he looked back he had already passed the white farm house. He quickened his pace and trotted along the road, dusty clouds puffed from the ground when each shoe struck the ground. Finally, he arrived at a small woodland where he stopped to look over the bay toward the City of Quincy for it was from the military airfield at Squantum those Corsair's had flown out from.

"I'm gonna do that some day." His voice was filled with excitement, "and I'm gonna fly a Corsair and I'm gonna go far out to sea," He held out his arms imitating a plane by banking first to the left and then right, "and I'm gonna see a German sub and come in low so's he doesn't see me and then, BAM! BAM! I'll drop my bombs right on it and kill all those Nazis. And they'll decorate me. And they'll call me a hero and I'll get a medal and....and...."

He spun in a huge circle, then stopped abruptly when he stared blankly. He balled his outstretched fists and dropped his arms to his sides. His lips moved imperceptibly while still mouthing the words, "BAM! BAM!" Suddenly, his eyes softened into a thoughtful look for he stared at a clearing where a white picket fence surrounded a miniature graveyard.

The gate creaked noisily when he stepped inside. He stood in the entrance tight lipped. His brow turned into a concerned frown when he glanced at the unfamiliar headstones, the creases in his forehead slowly disappeared from his open, youthful face. He read aloud the inscription of the only tombstone he recognized:

RALPH BENSON
BORN FEBRUARY 29, 1929
DIED JUNE 2, 1942

Peter sat on the ground next to Ralph's grave when from above a group of black crows filled the air with their obnoxious caws. The fleshy, ebony flight finally settled in trees to the boy's right, keeping up a constant chatter. The thirteen year old smiled warmly at the headstone and in moments he was staring meditatively in his strange surroundings.

The young boy wiped a tear with the back of his hand and then spoke softly at the marble stone, "Jeez, Ralph, I hate crows. They sound like they're always laughin' at me." He stretched himself so he lay prone to the grave, his eyes lingering at a fleeting white cloud that stood out starkly against a blue sky, clipping with the wind as it sped toward the outer harbor.

"I like watching clouds, Ralph, specially on a nice day, y'know, when there ain't much wind." He pointed to a cloud and continued, "They look like huge balloons, don't-cha think?"

Now repositioning himself he jammed his left elbow into the ground where he rested his head into his hand that found him now facing the grave. "I....I guess from where you're at you get to see all kinds of clouds. You're real lucky, Ralph." He flicked a stone off the top of the grave then sat crossed legged and continued his dialogue, "Well, I guess you want to know what's been happening? Well, I'm thirteen now. And Headmaster's got me workin' on the farm. I think he put me there cuz I got too friendly with his daughter Sheryl-Ann at the birthday table. She's real pretty. Anyway, the guys kinda pick on me. I think it's cuz I'm so small and all that."

He chuckled to himself, "You woulda laughed laughed at what happened in the cow barn. I....I fell into a whole bunch of cow shit. All the big kids laughed at me. My clothes had cow shit all over them." He snickered and hunched his shoulders, "But a big kid, Bix, kinda helped me. You'll like him. I'll....I'll bring him here to meet you some day, Ralph."

Blinking several times he continued, "I guess I'm gettin' as bad as you with all that swearing stuff." He warmed to his conversation. "This fall Coach Johnson's gonna let me play in the Pee-Wee Football league. I never played any sports before and I'm kinda scared. Oh! I'm hangin' 'round a kid called Feldman. He's not talkin' to me right now. Her's kinda mad cuz I gave him a nickname, Ike, and he didn't like it. Feldman's okay, though. He's kinda moody, but a nice guy."

"Oh yea, before I forget it, we're movin' in the new dorms next September. Just think Ralph, you and me could been roomates.

Suddenly, tears slipped down his cheeks, "Jeez Ralph, why didja go and die?" Wiping the tears away he drifted off in deep thought.

The tears flowed more freely when he said, "You....You was my best friend." He buried his face into his hands, sobs filled the small graveyard. He then stammered, "And I'm trying to stop this cryin stuff, but...but..."

From the gate a man's voice interrupted the boy's anguish. "Pappas. it's time to get back to the campus. Startled, Peter looked up in surprise. Armbrewster found him. The thirteen year old gulped deeply when he walked slowly toward the head farmer while wiping away tell-tale tears with the sleeve of his shirt.

Grim eyes followed the boy. "You left your assignment without permission, young man." The adult's voice was stern and demanding. "You also roamed the island without permission, didn't you?" Peter sneaked a quick look back at Ralph's grave and then turned to face his superior but did not answer.

"Come with me, young man." Armbrewster reached to place his arm around the boy's shoulders when the youngster pulled back in alarm The adult then spoke calmly, reassuringly, when he pushed his Panama hat back off his forehead, "We don't hit students at this school, young man." he comforted the boy's fears. "Now let's you and I get back to the main campus." He pointed toward a dirt path.

The Instructor became very serious as they walked along, "I guess you had a very special reason for breaking the second rule. You did wander the island without permission, didn't you?" Peter bowed his head and looked away for a moment. He then cast a quick look at his mentor, then silently looked down at his shoes. Finally, he broke his silence when he said, "I....I went to tell my friend Ralph about the things that've been happenin' to me." His face twisted sourly at the thought for he knew how ridiculous it must have sounded.

The thirteen year old looked up quickly and found himself looking directly into the sympathetic eyes of the Instructor. "Ralph's away now, Mister Armbrewster, Sir." His voice trailed off for he was still uncomfortable talking about such a sensitive subject. "He doesn't know unless I tell him." He hoped the adult would understand.

"Of course, Petee." Armbrewster's use of the boy's nickname was followed by a sudden clearing of his throat. "Of course," he repeated,

"Ralph should be told." he nodded his agreement. The two islanders started toward the main campus once again. Peter remained curiously quiet when the adult casually looked over the fields that were in various stages of harvesting.

A flock of noisy crows flew overhead, "They're laughin' at me." Peter mumbled as he watched them fly by.

The head farmer asked in surprise, "What did you say? Who's laughing at you?"

Embarrassed at his slip Peter chewed his lower lip, "Oh, it's those crows, Sir." He pointed at the birds swirling into a nearby grove of trees. "Whenever they're around they sound like they're laughin' at me. I'm getting to hate them." He shook his head in agreement.

A smile appeared on Armbrewster's face. He looked fondly at the young naive student, "Maybe they're laughing at me." He sat on a log by the side of the road and motioned for the boy to sit next to him. "You know, I've been on this island a lot longer than you and it just could be those crows know me better than they do you."

"Ya think so, Mister Armbrewster, Sir?" There was a hint of anxiety in the boy's voice. His concentration was firmly focused on the gaggle of ebony birds for he deep down he really had a fear of them.

"Crows are very smart birds, did you know that, Peter?" The boy shook his head negatively. "Did you ever read Edgar Allen Poe's, The Raven?"

"Yes, Sir." he responded quickly, "In school, Sir."

"Didn't you think the Raven was a smart bird?" "He sure was, Sir." he answered excitedly. "Well, the crow is related to the Raven, did you know that?" Before Peter could answer he continued, "If the crow has a hard piece of bread in its beak and it's too tough to eat he'll find some water and drop it in and then fly away. After a little while, when the bread is softened by the water the crow will come back and eat the bread. Now, isn't that petty smart? That's something you would do, isn't it?"

Suddenly, crows off to the left caught their attention. "Looks like they're fighting." Peter said when he saw the large brood scuffling over some food they uncovered. Armbrewster smiled at Peter's innocence and pointed at the birds. "See there, Petee." The boy looked in the direction, "See that one standing by himself?" he explained, "He's the one that gives warning to the others when there's danger coming their way." The youngster was captivated by the story. His excitement radiated when he said, "Jeez, Mister Armbrewster, those crows are as smart as us."

The Instructor was not finished educating his captive listener, "Suppose someone wanted to hurt you. What would you do?" "I'd probly hide, sir." he answered proudly.

"Your darn right you would. And that shows you how smart those Crows really are." He rubbed Peter's messed hair playfully and continued, "They certainly do hide."

"And the Crows are probly laughin' at the guy cuz he can't find em'. Huh, Mister Armbrewster, Sir?" The story teller smiled down on the boy and emphasized, "Yup! Probly."

"Gosh Mister Armbrewster," Peter pushed at a cowlick which dangled on his forehead, "Then those Crows probly ain't laughin' at me after all." He still had reservations about the Crows and felt safe in keeping that to himself.

They left the log and reached the road where Peter remembered that he had punishment coming too him. Finally, he asked hesitatingly, "I'm gonna get a demerit for what I did, huh, Mister Armbrewster, Sir."

The Instructor looked at his young charge. A wisp of a smile appeared on his face. When they passed the farm house the Peter glance wistfully in that direction for he wished he were there instead of finding out what demerits were waiting of him. Finally, his mentor said, "Don't you think you deserve two demerits - one for each of the things you did wrong today?"

Peter's lips pursed into a pout and then he answered meekly, "Well, maybe not big ones, Sir." He looked up at Armbrewster with hope fixed in his eyes. The farmer did not look at the boy for fear of giving away the chuckle he was suppressing, "Well, in my book these are pretty serious offences. If Headmaster Williamson finds out I didn't give you demerits then I'd be in trouble wouldn't it?"

"Yes, Sir." he answered, "I understand, Sir. I don't want you getting in trouble cuz of me, Sir."

Armbrewster nodded a smile. He then set his lips resolutely, placed his hat on his head and asked, "Let me toss this question to you, Mister Pappas. If you were in my shoes and you had to make a decision whether to give demerits, what would you do?"

The boy hunched his shoulders, "I don't know, Sir."

"Well, give it a try. Pretend you're me and you have to make a choice. Tell me what would you do?"

"Sir, I think...." he hesitated for a moment and then answered, "I'd stick with the rules. It would be two demerits. One for leaving my assignment and the other for roaming the island." He nodded his head in approval of his decision. But he really felt helpless that he had agreed to his punishment.

The adult pressed the point, "Even though it means two lost vacation days?"

The boy was uncomfortable with the conversation. He knew Armbrewster was leading up to something and he had better be careful how he answered. As if on cue noisy Crows flew directly overhead. "Yup." he said, "They're still laughin' at me. They're warning the others I'm around even though I ain't planning' on hurting 'em."

"You're probly right, son." The head farmer smiled condescendingly at the distracted teen. "And now that we've got all that out of the way how about if I only give you one demerit for leaving your assignment.?"

Peter's jaw dropped in surprise when he blurted, "Really, Sir? Oh, thank you, Sir."

Armbrewster chuckled, "That's the first time anyone thanked me for giving them a demerit."

"Yes, sir!" Peter gushed exuberantly, "I mean....Yes, Sir -I guess. Oh, I don't know what I'm saying, Sir." he chuckled at his own foolishness.

Before they parted Mister Armbrester asked, "You've been working on the farm for a few months now. How come someone your age is here when usually the boy's are older who do this kind of work?"

Peter felt uncomfortable with the question. He struggled for an answer and finally said,

"I know I'm kinda small, Mister Armbrewster, Sir, but....but I think I got stuck here cuz Headmaster Williamson caught me making eyes at his daughter Sheryl-Ann at the birthday table last September. And.... and poor Feldman nudged me and the Headmaster noticed and that's why Feldman's here too." He looked up at the smiling administrator and lowered his voice when he said, "I kinda like Sheryl-Ann and she even sits in front of me in seventh grade."

He focused on the ground when he finished by saying, "Sheryl-Ann's too young for me and I guess the Headmaster's making sure none of us guys get too friendly." Armbrewster patted the boy on the shoulder, then snickered by saying. "I guess you've learned a lesson in life, my boy."

CHAPTER SIX

THE ROMANTIC BULL

It was much later in the month when all the farm boys stood at the entrance to the barn waiting for their orders. The bays which held the hay were now restocked with the next years harvest. Cows were led to pasture as a daily routine. Lingering smells of dry hay drenched the air. The farm boys jostled each other in playful roughhousing for there was no one around in authority.

Bixby squatted to the side. He watched the others continue with their rough play. A young voice to his left asked, "Bix, d'ya think Mister Armbrewster's sick or sumpin?" The red head smiled when he recognized the voice. He moved over to make room for the squatting boy.

"Hi little kid," he acknowledged without taking his eyes off the roughhousing boys.

"Ya think Mister Armbrewster's sick or sumpin', Bix?" the boy repeated, "Is that why he ain't here yet?"

"Bixby nodded tight-lipped, "He might be, kid." Peter looked puzzled and asked, "Bix, did you forget my name?"

The senior answered quickly, "You're name's Ambercrombie." He nodded a smile at the surprised thirteen year old.

The boy giggled when he nudged the older boy with his elbow, "That's not my name." he defended.

Bix rubbed his chin as though was in deep thought and then said, "Nathaniel." He teased.

The boy's voice rose with excitement, "Common Bix, you know my name. I told you the day you showed me about the wheelbarrow."

"m-m-m-m, I guess your name should be," he hesitated for effect, "Hose-Nose!" he shouted.

Peter's laughter filled the barn. In one swift motion the burly youth pulled the screeching boy across his lap, then lifted his body high over his head. "You don't have a name." He yelled as he shook the exhilarated youngster high above his head.

"It's Petee," the boy's voice rose with the pitching of his body held by Bix's strong hands. "I'm Petee. I'm Petee." Bix dropped the squirming boy back on his lap, now holding the youthful face vice-like between his fingers and then imitated through a venomous smile, "A-A-Ahm, Peteeeeee! A-A-Ahm, Peteeeeee! A-A-Ahm a little squirt called Peteeeeee!"

Suddenly, a stern, authoritative voice interrupted the frenzied play, "Gentlemen, I want you to gather around me."

Headmaster Williamson scanned the crowding boys with a fixed scowl. He glared at Bixby who was setting Peter down. "Mister Armbrewster was called to the mainland last evening." he explained. "Because of his unexpected absence I shall take charge of the farm today. You will take your assignments from me and I expect a thorough job in whatever task you have to do."

Each student received his schedule for the day and rushed away. Peter continued to stand next to Bixby for he, Isaiah and Bixby had not been told what to do. Williamson frowned down on the two young boys and said, "You two will clean manure gutters today." The thirteen year old felt his heart plunge. He looked at Feldman who had squeezed his eyes shut behind his glasses.

"Bixby, you will help me. We've a cow that's to be sired." The order was demanding. The two teens turned and took very slow steps toward the dairy barn. Williamson rounded the corner of the barn and disappeared.

The cow barn was empty when Peter and Isaiah entered for the cows had been put to pasture. Silent and frustrated each boy took a wheelbrrow and shovel then began the unpleasant task. For an instant

Peter flashed back to his first day on the farm. The day he was humiliated with manure and milk. It was a catastrophe he would never forget.

He had to explain to Mr. Clifton who simply grinned at the boy's embarrassment. At thirteen years old he was ordered to strip his clothes while standing out of doors, the smell was putrid. His timing was off when the student body was released from early morning roll call and there they found the youngster completely naked where he shivered in the early morning dampness. The catcalls were bad enough, only he wondered what terrible new nicknames they would think up.

Peter instantly stopped shoveling when he heard a frantic, snorting bull bellowing from a locked private run next to the barn. The animal's prolonged bellow turned into bleating which instantly changed into deafening roars. The thirteen year old cast a troubled look at Feldman who had also stopped his work. The boys eyed each other now gripped in fear.

"What's that?" Peter asked when the bull charged the runway and slammed his horns that shuddered the side of the barn.

Feldman's face turned ashen. His lips were now tightened into a troubled pinch of fear. He dropped his shovel noisily on the cement floor and said, "I....I wonder if that bull's loose?"

"Ya think so? Ya think he's really loose?" Peter stared wide-eyed when Isaiah stared back with a frightened look. Peter took another quick look into the corridor leading to the bullpen. "I don't see any bull, but I see Bixby and Williamson down the hall with the cow."

"The noise, Petee. I made a lot of noise with the shovel." Isaiah was on the fringe of terror. "If that bull comes in here I'm running like hell."

Peter returned a alarmed look, "Are you crazy?" His eyes darted to the discarded shovel. Then a panic appeared on his face, "If that bull' loose he'll hear us and come for us." Looking confused the thirteen year old asked, "I wonder why they got that cow down there?" In seconds he formulated a solution to the unsettling question, "Maybe....Maybe it's the bull's mother. Maybe they got her there to keep the bull quiet."

Isaiah took a daring look down the corridor and said, "That bull's nuts! He's going craaazy!" He quickly retreated to the to the safety of the cow barn.

The youngsters huddled together with their shovels held across their chests in case they had to defend themselves. Suddenly, Bixby appeared at the entrance to the door of the corridor. The red head was saturated with perspiration. "Hey, you guys. We need your help." Peter's eyes bulged in fear. "Williamson's having a rough time with the bull and I can't control the cow and manage the gates at the same time."

"What! What do you want us to do about it?" Isaiah shouted in defense. "That bull's gonna kill us!"

The older boy's face turned red with rage. He jabbed his finger down the hall where the cow was mooing loudly. "Get your asses down there or so help I'm gonna throw you both into the bull's pen."

The two boys shifted numbed gazes which were filled with imploring, unanswerable questions. They slowly edged their way into the menacing corridor. Bixby led the way while explaining one of them had to hold the gate open when Williamson opened an outer gate to let the bull into its pen from the outside yard.

Bixby, in the meantime, would back the cow so its rump faced the frantic bull. Peter shouted above the raucous noise, "Is the bull gonna kill the cow? His face drained at the thought.

Exasperated with the questions the older boy shouted orders, "Petee, you help me hold the cow. Feldman, stand by the inner gate in case the bull gets loose and be ready to let us out if that happens." The youngsters exchanged quick horrified looks, then entered the hall where the cow's impassioned cries deafened them.

From the outer yard the bull's menacing horns struck the bars desperately. "Is everyone in position?" Williamson shouted above the roars of the bull. He shimmied a long pole to the outer gate's lock. Bixby and Peter had maneuvered the bellowing cow so the rump was jutting just inside the vacant bull's pen. Bedlam filled the barn with the two animals howling together. The pole released the locking mechanism. Suddenly, the outer gate flew open when the frustrated bull charged. The inner walls vibrated when the pen instantly filled with a ton of brute male passion. Peter froze at the sight of the massive animal who was now obsessed by the tantalizing rump of the begging cow. The massive bull pulled up on his hind legs and lunged to penetrate his rousing mate.

"The bull's hurting her!" Peter yelled where his eyes were riveted on the monstrous brute who's mass filled the whole pen.

The limited enclosure now found the cow trying to back herself into the bull's pen, however, Bixby stood his ground by hauling back on the halter on the cow's neck. Now the bull was having problems positioning himself. Saliva drooled from its mouth when he aimed to enter the cow.

He thrust mightily, but his penis missed the cow's vulva - a stream of ejaculation erupted forward. Bixby seeing the episode had no room to dodge the oncoming deluge. The repugnant stream struck him squarely in the face, blinding him with the goo. It was impossible for the red head to avoid a second failed ejaculation and with this the muscular red head yelled at his displeasure.

"What's that stuff?" A stunned Peter asked. Bixby ignored the boy when he continued his struggle with the cow. Williamson raced into the chamber and jabbed a pole at the menacing bull while the cow was extricated. The inflamed bull continued to furiously attack the bars on either side of the cow.. Finally, when the bull retreated from Williamson's pole the gate was slammed shut with the suffering bull groaning in misery.

Now roaring at its failure the mighty bull once again assaulted the rigid bars.. The two young boy's mouths gaped at the bewildering events when Bixby led the decimated cow out to pasture. She quickly bolted away only to suddenly stop and furiously churn the soil with her hoofs. From a distance a frustrated bull continued to bellow loudly, now filling the entire barn area with his failed priority.

"Jeez, didja ever see somthin like that?" Peter spoke to himself. His face paled from all the excitement.

Feldman pulled his glasses from his face and wiped his brow with a handkerchief, "Bixby's gonna be pissed with all that sperm all over him."

Peter then questioned, "Sperm, what's that?" he was ignored, "What's that you called it, Isaiah? Sperm?" He pressed for an answer. "Tell me, Feldman? What's this sperm stuff?"

Peter's friend took a quick look at the inquisitive youth and asked, "Didn'cha ever hear of sperm?" His dark eyes narrowed at the innocence of the questioner. "Petee, don'tcha know that's the stuff that makes babies?" The thirteen year old hunched his shoulders. He almost wished he never asked the question because it made him feel so ignorant. But, he was inquisitive. He needed an answer since was something new to him.

"I don't know about babies, Ike." he confessed, "I guess I'm kinda stupid."

Feldman got right to the point, "Did ya see how hard the bull's dong was?" he asked.

"Yea," the boy answered with an overwhelming sense of ignorance.

"Didn'cha see the bull stick it inside the cow?"

"Yea, but, I....L..." he let the sentence drop. A blush filled his cheeks.

Feldman's exasperation mounted, "When the bull sticks his dong into the cow he shoots the sperm into her and it mixes with stuff inside the cow and after awhile a baby cow is born."

Peter was stunned, "Well I don't' see no baby cow, Ike."

"Oh fer chriz-sake Petee. You're real dumb!" The intolerant Feldman slammed his shovel on the cement floor and punched at an imaginary person. "Petee!" he shouted, "I just told you it takes a while before the baby cow gets here. It's probably weeks from now or....or even months from now."

Peter shifted his numbed gaze from Feldman to Bixby who was wiping his face by the pasture gate. The youngster turned back to his friend and asked, "But why did the bull's dong get so big?"

"Jeezus, Petee!" Isaiah looked at his friend incredulously, "Doesn't your dong get hard sometime?"

Peter blushed, then turned away. He started toward his wheelbarrow with his tutor close behind him waiting for an answer. "Petee, doesn't your thing get hard sometimes?" The knowledgeable Isaiah persisted with his question. The thirteen year old picked up his shovel and twisted its handle so the metal point spun in the wheelbarrow. "Sometimes." The answer was a whisper, "But I don't know why." He avoided looking at Isaiah.

Feldman pressed the issue for he knew his friend had to have this explained to him. "Didn't you ever have sperm come out of your dong when it's hard."

The answer was slow in coming. The thirteen year old was uncomfortable with the conversation, but he was still curious. Finally, he answered, "One night I dreamed I was in a rowboat. The sea was pretty rough with the waves splashing me. My friend Ralph was near the bow of the boat and he was pulling the oars. I sat at the stern -you know, where the little seat is. Well, in my dream Ralph thought he was being funny by turning the boat into the waves. He knew I couldn't swim and he was laughin' at me. I kept yelling at him to get us back to the dock, but, the more I yelled the more he laughed. All of a sudden a big wave came over the bow of the boat and it swished right passed Ralph. The water came right at me and I was screaming cuz I was scared. And then that icy water hit me. And that's when it happened.

Peter squirmed as he related the story. He bowed his head when he saw a simple smile on Isaiah's face. "I woke up," he continued, "and all this wet stuff was leaking out of my....my....thing. I thought my insides was coming out of me." He faced his wheelbarrow, turning his back on his friend, "I was real scared, Ike."

I didn't tell anyone. I didn't know what that stuff was and I thought for sure something bad was happening to me." The youngster turned abruptly and faced Feldman. "Was that sperm, Isaiah?"

Peter's understanding friend chuckled, "You had a wet dream, that's all. It can happen to anyone. Was that your first one?"

A hesitant reply answered, "Yea."

"Did you like it?"

"Yea, I think. It made me feel nice but gooey wet."

"Petee," Ike continued, "Did you ever hear the guys talking about playing with themselves?"

"Well, yea, but" he set his lips resolutely and answered simply, "I didn't know what they wuz talkin' about."

Feldman jammed his hand to his forehad and said, "Well, ya gotta learn some time." He started to the rear of the barn. When he reached the large door he called Peter to join him. The two boys disappeared into the darkness.

Time passed and the two friends suddenly reappeared. Peter's lips were raised into a half smile and silently returned to his wheelbarrow. Feldman shouted, "Hey, Petee, didja like it?" The thirteen year old gave him a tight, wry, mischievous smile and then that smile radiated brightly, "Yea," he answered, I liked it. I liked it a lot."

CHAPTER SEVEN

KING PHILIP'S WAR

The main harbor channel was filled with ships forming yet another convoy housing troops going to war in Europe. Peter watched solemnly where he sat just beyond the north end goal of the football field. He wondered which of his remaining brothers might be on board. His oldest brother Lou was already in Africa with U.S. troops embroiled in heated battles against General Rommel's German troops.

The news reports were filled with staggering clashes to halt the "Desert Fox" as the German General was called.

Another brother had entered that part of the service where letters could be written to him, but he was not able to answer because he was involved in some kind of clandestine operation for the military. The teenager fantasized his brother John's exploits at some adventure of spying, or being a saboteur, or maybe hiding in the hills of a foreign country training gorilla's or partisan's for a secret clandestine operation. After the war these fantasies turned out to be true.

Two other brothers remained stateside and the youngster was prepared to hear that they too left our safe harbor. He turned to his right from his vantage point at the north end of the island where he could see tug boats sweep back the submarine nets so the giant ships could pass and enter the North Sea.

Seated next to him Isaiah Feldman complained how quickly the weather had turned so very cold. They had been through winter storms on the island in other years and each of the fourteen year olds dreaded the thought that an island sticking out of the ocean would be battered once again. Feldman tugged at his coat if only to make himself believe it was enough to take the chill out. His breath curled with steam when he tossed rocks down the bluff which ended at the rocky beach below. "Jeez, Ike." Peter seemed disturbed with his thoughts, "I wish I was old enough to go to war like my brothers."

Feldman also pitched a rock which careened noisily belween two large boulders at the base of the precipice. "Hey, Petee, don't rush it." he advised, "When they start drafting us fourteen year olds it means we're losing the war."

Peter smiled when he was about to answer only to be suddenly interrupted with the arrival of Bixby who broke through the brush and squatted obtrusively between the two friends. "Guess what?" he asked in a voice filled with excitement. "Headmaster's letting a bunch of us eighteen year olds go and enlist - I'm heading for the submarines."

Peter's brow knit into a frown, "You mean you're going to war, Bix?" A startled expression filled his face.

Feldman, about to lob another stone stopped his throw in midair, "Talk about pissin' your pants." He finally completed the toss when he facetiously said, "Yea, those subs fill up real fast - and then, squish."

He clutched his throat pretending to gasp for air, "Gurgle, gurgle and you're gone. You're dead."

"Cut it out, Ike!" Peter snapped, "That's not funny." Bixby ignored the comment when he lay back on his elbows while casting a long look at the transports forming in the harbor. "See those troop ships out there? Well, I'm the guy that's gonna protect them." He thrust his finger at Feldman, "And guys like you, Ike, better pray I'm out there."

Isaiah pulled away in mock surprise, "Hey, you don't think I'm gonna get into this war? I've got news for you. This kid's not going anywhere to get himself killed."

Peter leveled a callous smile at his friend and snapped, "Damn, Ike! If they draft you, you're gonna go wherever Uncle Sam wants you." He smiled bitterly, "And if Uncle wants you dead, you're gonna be dead and that's it!"

The burly red head chuckled at the outburst, "You guys ain't gonna see any war, so what the hell are ya talkin' that way? He turned his attention to Peter, "What are you, fourteen? Fifteen? He was more conciliatory to the youngsters, "By the time you're old enough this war's gonn be over - so what the hell are ya both talkin' about?"

Peter hunched his shoulders. He grasped a handful of loose soil and scattered it down the bluff. "I'm only fourteen." he answered softly.

"See what I mean?" Bixby continued, "it's gonna be four years before you turn eighteen. And eighteen is the draft age." He shook his head, "You guys ain't never gonna get in this war." There was a finality in his voice.

Peter stared down in a pout, "Yea, but what about you, Bix?" he asked, "When are you leaving?"

Bixby's voice was full of excitement when he answered, "Tomorrow afternoon I'm enlisting in the Navy. I'm volunteering for submarines right away." He flashed a toothy smile at the boys. Peter turned and faced the husky red head. A gentle, concerned gaze was fixed on his face. He then faced away, now frowning at the mass of ships in formation. "Will ya write me, Bix?" he asked above a whisper.

Bixby smiled at his young friend and answered, "Well, the letters might be a bit wet." He winked and continued, "Don't forget, water fills subs pretty fast." He stood and waved goodbye.

Time had passed when the winter winds brought snow and hail to the islanders. The classes and the work schedule were so routine that boredom soon crept in. With a heavier than usual snowfall that year in 1943, winds cut a swath across the island, laying what looked like a white cushion that covered the north end to the south end. Preparations had been well planned for the barn was full of hay and various grains filled the bins to capacity. There were assurances the horses, cows, pigs and chickens would do well that year.

Peter stood by the window in the infirmary in Bowditch House where he was recovering from a flu that had cut him to the quick. His view took in the football field where students carved huge chunks of snow and soaked them with water until they froze solid. He watched the boys place the heavy ice encrusted snow blocks in a rectangle outlying the beginnings of a snow fort.

At the other end of the football field a second group was building a comparable fort. He was on the second floor of Bowditch House, the same building which housed the dining room on the first floor.

It had been a tormenting time for the youth who finally seemed to be recovering from the illness which savaged the entire school. It was his turn now and finally he felt well enough to hope they would release him.

He shared the infirmary with three other boys who were also confined as a result of the damnable flu. The isolation was just too complete. "Jeez, I wish I could get out of here." He spoke to the other boys who paid no attention to him for in their confinement for they were happy to escape the daily rigors of the school's schedule, they languished in their temporary freedom.

He whispered to himself, "Pretty soon they'll be having King Philip's War and I'll be stuck here watching from this darn window."

"It's too damned cold to be playing Indians and Settlers." A voice spoke from the door. Peter took a quick look over his shoulder and smiled broadly at his friend Isaiah who had pulled off his heavy winter coat and sprawled himself on Peter's empty bed. "Wish I could spend a few days up here. I'd make sure they kept me for weeks and weeks." He tucked his hands under his head and gazed at the ceiling through steamed glasses.

Peter straddled the end of the bed while shoving Feldman's boots to one side. "Why are you dirtying my bed? he snapped while squirming to untangle his robe from around his waist. "You're boots smell like horse-shit." he complained.

Isaiah propped on his elbows pulled the pillow behind his head. Smirking wryly he answered, "Of course they stink. I purposely brought them so you wouldn't forget what the farm smells like. Peter cast a sweet, venomous smile at his friend, "Well, I've got a surprise for ya. Headmaster's taking me off the farm, so where does that grab ya?"

Feldman's eyes widened with interest. He twisted off the bed and sat on the edge with Peter beside him. "Well, two bits you end up with the Coach in landscaping. You always were his pet."

Peter gave his friend a tense look, "And how did you know I'd be working for the Coach? I just found out yesterday."

"You can't keep secrets in a school like this. Besides," he stuck his nose in the air and finished with an uppity smile, "I've got Jewish spies everywhere."

"Well. I think I'd like mowing lawns instead of shoveling cow shit and the rest of that farm stuff."

"Yea, and in winter you're gonna feeze your ass off shoveling snow." The visitor lay back into the pillow, then met the gaze of his friend, "It's as tough as farm work, ya know."

"That's okay, Ike. At least I'll be doin' something I like," he hesitated, "and besides, I like Coach." Peter's ally took a large chocolate bar from his coat and tossed it to Peter. "Here, that's for you."

Peter smiled at the gift, "Gees, Ike, thanks a lot. But, you're so cheap, how come this? Yuk! Yuk!" he retorted while unwrapping it.

"Cuz you're a sicko and I hope it gives you cavities! Yuk! Yuk! yourself."

"Sounds like you're pissed at me." He said while offering his friend some chocolate.

"Naa, I'm not pissed at you. I thought we'd still be working together on the farm, that's all.

Peter wiggled closer while licking chocolate from his fingers, "We'll be seeing each other in class and in sports and the band stuff."

Feldman snapped off another chew of the candy. His lips were now covered by the softened treat when he suddenly smiled brightly showing teeth plugged brown with chocolate. Peter screeched in delight, "You look like you got rotten teeth."

"Oh yea," Feldman yelped when he lunged at Peter and shoved his chocolate coated hand into Peter's face smearing his pale skin. "Now you look like real cow shit." His antagonist snapped.

"And you smell like cow shit, Feldman.." The boy retorted when he too lunged at Ike and ground the remaining candy bar into his visitor's hair. In seconds the two friends crashed into one another, tumbling on the bed in a wrestling frenzy. Their laughter filled the room when the two plunged to the floor in a madcap array of arms and legs recklessly gripped upon each other. Finally, the heavier Isaiah pinned his weaker adversary. Their faces but inches apart they both struggled to catch their breath.

She stood by the opened door. A petite woman whose round face was accented by gray penetrating eyes. All the boys knew she wore an auburn wig which hid an unknown disease that caused her to be hairless. She nodded tight-lipped at the two boys sprawled on the floor,

"Mister Pappas, the infirmary is no place to be roughhousing." She jammed her hands into the pockets of her stiff hospital uniform and scowled down at the two boys. "And you, Mister Feldman, should know better than to create mischief.

Feldman slipped off the prostrate Peter and knelt next to his friend. "I'm sorry, Miss Parkway." he answered as he sucked the chocolate from his fingers. "Petee and me was just foolin' round." A red blush filled his cheeks.

"Pette and 'I were' just fooling around." she corrected the poor grammar.

The petite nurse took Peter's wrist and timed his pulse. Her brow wrinkled into a frown while the boy looked at her anxiously. "I'm okay, ain't I, Miss Parkway." Her gray eyes peered down on the boy. "Your pulse is very rapid, young man." she cautioned, "If you keep this up you're going to be here a lot longer than you expect. She cast a questioning look at the boy and shook her head "And what's all that goo on your hands? Your face is covered with it. You're filthy, young man and it's a shower for you right now."

The two boys gave each other tense looks and then snickered, "It smells like chocolate, Ma'am." But the stern woman was already wetting a face cloth and began scrubbing Peter's face. "I can do it, Miss Parkway." Peter protested when he tried to pull away. But the nurse was adamant so she would teach him a lesson. "If you want to act like a child I may as well treat you as one." Feldman quickly tried to clean the chocolate off himself, then smiled his innocence at the tight-lipped governess hovering over the struggling boy.

"But I get tired of just hanging around." Peter complained. He frowned in protest, but gave her a quick, uneasy smile when she finally finished.

She looked as if she were angry when suddenly she smiled fondly, "You've been doing very well in the mending department, young man. If we can keep the chains on you I think you'll be out of here in time for that terrible King Philips War." Her eyes rolled to the ceiling when she said, "And God help us with all those bruises and cuts and hurts." She said as she left the room.

Suddenly Coach Johnson entered the room now looking at Peter with a look hidden in surprise. "You were picked for one of the teams,

Petee." The voice startled Peter when he turned to face the big man. A smile filled the boy's face when the Coach continued, "Looks like you're an Indian."

The words tumbled out of the boy's mouth, "I'm gonna paint my face with red stripes," Coach Johnson, "And....And I'll carry a tomahawk. And I'll be like Bix. I'll be just as tough as Bix." His voice trailed off when he became serious and asked, "Will Bix be here for the war? Will he come visit in his sumbarine uniform?"

The Coach's face lost it's smile when he explained, "Petee, Bix had an accident when training for the subs." Peter stared anxiously at the sudden ominous news. Johnson stepped closer to the boy and said, "Petee, Bix is blind." A shudder shook the young boy's shoulders. "While training in a sub mock-up a steam pipe burst. Bix saved the lives of the others by trying to block a broken gushing steam pipe." The Coach continued. Petee, Bix is a hero."

Peter looked directly into the Coach's eyes and then turned away. His shoulders sagged when he finally said, "Leave it to Bix." His voice trailed off when he buried his face into his hands and wept.

Finally, he turned back to the Coach when wiping away tears and said, "Bix is my friend, you know." He looked over at his confident Ike who was still standing by the window wiping his glasses. The distraught boy continued, "Bix is the kind of guy who'd volunteer for all the dangerous jobs." He nodded his head in agreement with himself.

"He did the same thing when he was here, didn't he, Petee?" Ike broke the silence in the room. He looked over at his heartbroken friend and continued, "Remember that time in the barn with the cow and the bull? It was Bix who fought with the cow and was only inches away from those horns on the charging bull."

Peter chuckled and answered, "Yea, and me and you were scared as hell." He smiled at the Coach who had draped his arm around the miserable youth. The athletic director squeezed the youngsters shoulders and said, "That's the way you guys should remember Bix." He turned and left the room.

It was days later when the shock of Bix's accident slowly found its way into the back of Peter's mind. Now out of the infirmary he was planning what his role should be in King Philip's War. He had formulated plans to attack the Settlers fort and kick a corner of their fort with a hope he would not get caught and then weaken the corner and in no time would have the whole fort tumbling down and all the points would go to his team.

But was he strong enough after being sick? He remembered the Coach warning him if he did not think Peter was strong enough he was not going to let him join the Indians and he would have to watch from the side lines, This would be a calamity for the ambitious boy. He was bound and determined to prove his ability.

He knew that the few days remaining before the war would give him a chance to rush to the gym and begin preparing to build his stamina. It was a grueling task when he lifted weights and pulled on chest weights to develop his muscles. Running the track proved he was not really prepared for he found himself winded after a few laps. He was so glad there were no other students watching him.

He heard from others who had participated in this war last year that the young kids would be tossed about like ping pong balls. They would be pitched up toward the edge of the eight foot walls where the defenders protected their bags by placing two or three guards who would ambush anyone getting up that far.

Beefy Settler football players would forge alliances to tangle Indian beefy football players at the base of the fort and since anything goes except fist fighting it was sure to be something dreadful for the younger boys. Since this was Peter's first time at this grueling adventure his spirits tended to plummet, however, he was bound and determined to give it all he could.

Since he had two days to get himself in shape he felt more confident in his abilities. He wished Ike was with him to go through gymnastic routines, but his friend was down with the flu and in the infirmary. Although Ike did not like much of physical contact sports he often did his best to hold up his end and refused to show any weakness in anything he tried. This was an important reason why they bonded as friends.

Washington's Birthday was the day of King Philip's War. It was named after an Indian who caused havoc amongst the Pilgrim Settlers in Plymouth, Massachusetts during the sixteen hundreds. But now, the historical significance was a footnote in this modern day. Down on the bitter cold field the entire student body was gathering.

Feldman, who was allowed to leave the infirmary and here found Peter's friend bundled with heavy blankets which offered him some comfort from the north wind's bite. He saw the Coach standing on a bench telling the boys that anything was allowed in the attack from tackling to shoving to piling on one another. Ike looked for his friend Peter and finally found the seventh grader appearing so frail next to the burly combatants.

Fist fighting would not be tolerated, the Coach explained, and the offenders would be ejected. The boys painted as Indians would be the first to attack the Settler's fort and try to remove coded bags which were secured within the ice fort. Each confiscated bag deposited into the Indian fort held certain numerical values and therefore would count against the defenders.

After thirty minutes of the first skirmish the coded bags would be placed in the Indian's fort and the same rules applied. Since each fort was guarded by half the student body it seemed unlikely bags could be seized, however, ingenuity often prevailed. At the end of the two attacks the coded bags would then be lined to between the two forts and then a crushing dash between the two hostiles to grab as many bags as they could and get them into their own forts. It promised to be a grueling battle.

Because Feldman was recently released from the infirmary he was not allowed to participate. Looking down from his vantage point the could make out his friend Petee, his face painted like an Indian, mingling with the others. His heart raced when the whistle signaled the attack. Whooping cries filled the air when the advancing Indians charged headlong at the defending Settler's fort.

Maneuvers proved fruitless when Settler combatants guarding the bags at the top of the fort hurled ice encrusted balls of snow at the encroaching Indians. Well worked out plans by the Indians met a stone wall of Settlers defending the base. There was an instant clash of bodies slipping on packed snow crushed by the wall of defenders. Somewhere in the tangled mass Petee met with other tribesmen where he was boosted like a sling-shot to the top of the Settlers fort.

It was a smart plan, however, the defenders on the top of the fort ruthlessly bashed the youngster by plunging snow barriers right into the charging youngster's face. It foiled the plan when Pete fell back to the ground into the mass below, but, their struggle was just beginning when the advancing Indians charged headlong at the defending Settlers. Despite well worked out plans the Indians failed in their attempts to shove younger boys into the top of the fort. Scrawny young Indians were tossed around like playthings.

Beefy Settler football players formed a ring of brute force, however, the slippery snow did not offer any foothold and in moments a tangled web of Settlers and Indians lay sprawled at the base of the fort. It was a valiant struggle between both teams and for the moment none of the striped bags from the Settlers fort had been lost to the Indians.

Feldman yelled excitedly when he saw Peter heaved up the side of the ice encrusted fort only to see his friend unceremoniously tumble to the base. Yells from the top defenders signaled a youth had managed to invade the bag sanctuary and manged to toss out five bags to his companions below. Bedlam exploded by the Settlers when those same bags were heaved mid-field forcing the Settlers to split their forces in first defending their fort and second to retrieve the loose mid-field bags. The Settlers suddenly found their defenses weakened.

A reckless scramble for the loose bags brought each team in a frenzied effort at capture. Two bags were cleverly pitched toward the Indian fort which landed even closer now offering a better postion to get them inside the attackers fort. With the Settlers forces now split the Indians intensified their efforts and put more pressure on the defenders.

A deluge of youngster were now overwhelming the top defenders for it was easier for the Indians to distract the beefy protectors so they could carry out their offensive deployment. With more striped bags being heaved off the Settlers fort freewheeling Indians grabbed the bags and raced them to their fort to get them inside so they would count.

Peter, in the meantime, had secured himself at a corner of the Settlers fort and began kicking the icy corner away which exposed looser snow from within. Still unseen by the defenders the youth kicked savagely where larger chuncks were weakening that one corner. But, that small victory to bring down that corner was only momentary when he was discovered and pounced upon by two of the bigger Settlers. His bravery was rewarded by being stuffed into a snow bank where he finally crawled out the other side. Finally, a whistle blew shrilly ending the first phase.

Feldman's voice was getting hoarse fom the verbal support he was giving his friend. Suddenly. Pater raced to him, "Didja see me, Ike?" His excitement radiated, "Didja see me throw the bags out of the Settler's fort?" Feldman tried to answer, but his friend's enthusiasm was overwhelming, "I did it, Ike. I did it all by myself." Of course he overlooked the help he got from his allies in pitching him up and over the eight foot wall of ice. It would be later when the excitement of the day wore off that he would agree it took teamwork. But for now, with his clothes caked in ice, he raced back to the field of play.

"The Indian's have two five's and two fifteens," Coach Johnson shouted across the field to all the combatants, "That makes the Indians leading by forty points." A group cheer resounded from the Indian fort which was met by menacing glares from the subdued Settlers. Finally, the Settler's lined up for an attack against the Indians.

There was a sense of desipereation that filled the voices of the charging Settlers. The defenders braced for what was sure to be a grueling onslaught. The Settlers were swift and cunning when all of the attacking Settlers converged on all four corners of the enemies fort, thus forcing the defenders to split their forces to the four corners. It was a sly, well worked out attack plan, for well placed kicks to each corner chiseled away at the base of the stronghold. The Indians immediately grasped the intention of the invaders plan pounced on the intruders with savage fury, forcing the aggressive attackers back momentarily. Adrenaline reached fever pitch from both sides, but the abuse the fort was receiving at each corner was having a disastrous affect.

Weaknesses in the Indian forts structure was proving that the fort was not as well built as the boys had assumed. Now, melting snow at the base of the fort found all of the youthful combatants slipping and falling in slush. The adversaries kept kicking the foundation until chunks of ice covered snow fell away from the corners. Crumbling corners uncovered the softer snow the ice had covered and now huge gaps were threatening to tumble the eight foot flaking columns.

Whoever came up with this brilliant plan was certainly going to be idolized by the challengers. Suddenly, from above, a voice rose shrilly, "They're up here! They climbed up the back! Guards at the top of the fort grappled with the invaders, but it was too late. Multiple striped bags filled the air where they were tossed freely by the hoard who infiltrated the bulwark. The Indians were now in desperation. Their fort was crumbling. Prized striped bags were loose in the field of play where the Settlers scooped them and rushed back to their own fort so they would count against their enemy.

The attack became a frenzy; a blur of youthful teens anxiously defending what seemed a failing cause. The aggressive Settlers failed to see a lonely figure scurrying through deep snow along the edge of the battlefield. From the sidelines Feldman could not believe his eyes when he observed his friend Petee crawling unseen toward the Settlers fort. He clapped his hand over his mouth to stop a shout of encouragement he wanted to give the aggressive teen.

Numbing cold gripped the youngster who had successfully arrived at the rear of the unprotected Settlers fort. Except for two Settlers who manned the top of the fort to retrieve captured bags tossed up to them Petee felt secure his plan of attack would work. With his boot he chipped a toe hole into the ice encrusted wall, then slid numbed fingers into crevices and slowly inched his way upward.

Peter chewed his bottom lip as the stress of what he was about to do magnified the thrill he was experiencing. He was now clawing at even smaller ice filled chink holes which quickly helped him maneuver closer to the top. From this risky position he could hear the two boys inside the top of the fort speaking excitedly about their comrades successes at the Indian fort. He knew they would not be paying any attention to what was happening behind them. It was a perfect distraction, if only.... if only he could slip over the edge and into the treasure trove of captured Indian bags without making any sounds.

Finally, he rounded his body over the top of the enemies fort. His heart pounded in exhilaration where he locked his eyes on the backs of the two guards who were distracted by the melee going on at the far end of the field. In rapid succession Petee tossed captured bags over the back of the fort anticipating escaping to gather the ill-gotten goods once he fled.

Suddenly, his two adversaries pounced on the distracted youth, pinioning him with the weight of their combined bodies. The renegade Indian struggled with all of his might, but it was useless, his efforts to sneak in unnoticed sapped his strength, he was too weak to defend himself. "You're not such a smart-ass, Petee Pappas." one boy snarled into the upturned face of the helpless boy. "We knew you were coming and we set this trap for you." Peter winced at the thought that all of his efforts were for nothing.

"Now we're gonna give you a royal Settler send-off." The second boy snarled through clenched teeth."

They hauled the diminished Indian to his feet, then stuffed the back of his shirt with loose snow. Peter grimaced when the frigid melting snow slid down to his waist. But, he was not about to show any sign of defeat when he tried to pull loose; it was hopeless when he was yanked by his wrists and hauled to the rear of the structure. "You've had it now, Indian boy." his adversaries laughed cruelly at the thought of their demonic plan was unfolding.

Peter gulped deeply when he was forced over the edge of the eight foot wall and stared down at the heaped snow left over from the forts construction. "And over you go, hero." In one motion Peter was lifted over the ledge and found himself airborne, now flailing the air in his speedy plunge into a massive snow mound.

He scrambled off the snow pile and took a solemn look at the loose bags he managed to throw out of the Settlers fort. From above the two adversaries grinned down upon him, one of whom snarled, "Don't even think of taking those away, Chief Pow Wow." They laughed down upon the demoralized boy, for he knew if he attempted to grab any of the bags he would have to fight the two defenders once again. He just didn't have the strength to take them on.

Now drenched from the melting snow on his clothes he unfastened his pants and released the soggy snow which had also melted between his shirt and his skin. It was an instant relief to be rid of the soaking mess. Trudging slowly through the battlefield filled with crunchy snow he chastised himself for not succeeding in his mission. Looking into the distance he suddenly became very aware his teammates needed him in the grueling battle at his own fort. There was no time to feel sorry for himself.

Two well aimed snowballs barely missed him when his protagonists continued to taunt the retreating teen. Finally, a sharp whistle ended the conflict at the Indian fort, for it was time to begin the third phase of King Philip's War, Peter rushed to return and dismissed the failure he had experienced. Coach Johnson counted each forts prized bags and announced sixty-five points for the Settlers and eighty-five points for the Indians. The dumbfounded Settlers looked in awe at the thought they were losing.

A tempest of Indian whoops filled the air which were instantly followed by stomping feet imitating an Indian victory dance. It was a grinning Peter who wrapped himself into the excitement for now all thoughts of his failed foray was quickly dismissed. When he looked at his own fort it looked just like disaster had completely altered its shape. But this was no time to worry about that for the triumph could still be lost in the final stage of this war.

All of the bags were now laid in a single row across the center dividing the two forts. Each team stood in front of their respective forts for at Coaches signal they would charge and scoop bags and return them to their fort for the points to count. It promised to be a ferocious confrontation. Tension filled the air. Each team knew they could win or lose this war by what was about to happen at mid-field.

All of the boys looked rag-tagged, soaked through their clothes from the combat. Hearts beat as one when the two groups lined up in front their own forts. Suddenly, a cutting whistle signaled the attack to begin. Like a pulsating wave in motion the students streaked toward the bags which were stretched mid-field. The Indian team shrieked war whoops as a call to victory.

The two belligerents clashed in mid-field. Eager hands gripped the prized bags with their stripes indicating point value only to be attacked by the enemy thus tearing them away. Bags flew to the rear where reserves rushed them back to their own forts so they would count. Peter clutched two bags, turned to flee and was instantly tackled. Not being heavy his frail frame was instantly smothered by two football players - the boy had no chance.

It only took minutes for the field to be cleared of the precious bags. Each group, Settler and Indian guarded their loot when suddenly the Indians, in a calculated plan, descended upon the Settlers fort placing the their enemy of the defensive. From behind a small contingent of Indians guarded their own fort. It was a well directed ploy to keep the Settlers away from the warriors defenses.

But, the maneuver only worked for a few minutes when shouts from the Indian fortress announced that they too were under attack. Immediately the attacking Indians now became the defenders when they raced back to protect their clutch of bags. Petee hung back when both sides became embroiled in another major battle. The teenager anticipated the guards in the Settler's fort would be distracted with what was happening at the other end of the field.

He scaled the back of the Settlers fort once again and was about slip inside when suddenly a grinning face stared down on him. The defender held a huge snow ball above his head menacingly. Peter smiled up sheepishly. His fingers were loosing their grip on the slippery surface and there he dangled precariously. "You don't give up, do you Petee." The adversary crushed the frigid snow squarely into the teens face where the boy lost his grip and like a tumbling Raggedy-Ann doll fell helplessly to the bottom.

At that moment a sharp whistle announced the end of the notorious King Philip's War. It was time to see who won. A subdued gathering of Indians stood breathlessly waiting the outcome of the count. Coach Johnson along with Mister Clifton counted the value of each striped bag taken from the Indian's fort. Peter squatted on a chunk of ice where he tugged at his clothes to remove the particles of snow that was now melting. He shook himself like a dog shaking its fur. Feldman had come up behind his friend and said, "Those big guys didn't take any mercy on you or any of the other smaller guys. Gees, I thought they were sure gonna break your arm or something." Peter smiled at his concern and answered, "Yea, for now we're little guys. But wait 'til I grow up, then it'll be my turn. I'll blast their heads off." he chuckled at his own attempt at bravery.

Coach Johnson returned from the Settlers fort holding a pad notated with figures and announced: "One hundred fifteen points for the Indians." A cheer from the hopeful Indians brought hoots and stomping feet into a parody of war dances. Then, a hush fell over the assembly. "One hundred twenty points for the winning Settlers." The winning announcement brought a roar from the Settlers.

"Missed it by five points." Peter said when he kicked a small snow pile. If only I could have gotten into that fort." he looked at Feldman and smiled thinly, "I guess there's got to be a loser, huh."

The Settlers moved off to the gym where hot cocoa and snacks awaited the winning team. Still dripping from his drenching, Peter stood outside the door to the gym where his team of Indians awaited the invitation which was always extended by the winning team to the losers. In a short time the Indians were ushered to the waiting snacks amid boo's and cat calls from the winners.

Peter slid onto a bench where he sat quietly by himself until his friend Feldman joined him. The two boys reinvented the days events -Peter's eyes glistened when he retold how he almost captured striped bags from under the very noses of the opponents. He pressed his back against the wall and drifted off in thought. "Hey, Petee, what're you thinking about?" His friend asked.

"Oh, I was thinking if Bix was on our side how we would have won. He was a real strong guy."

Feldman fell silent for a moment for he noticed there was tense, haggard look coming from Peter. He knew his friend was struggling with some unexplained internal turmoil . Peter spoke as if he were alone. As if there was an unseen spirit somewhere around who was listening to him, "First it's Ralph and then it was Bix.' Feldman looked at him curiously and for some reason did not bother to interrupt his friend. Peter sucked in his breath, then rested his head against the brick gym wall. Shutting his eyes for a moment he continued, "I guess it's me. It's gotta be me."

Feldman looked at Peter with troubled, shifting eyes. He gave a quick look around the gym noticing that no one was paying attention to them. He was glad that they were alone. He was totally confused when he placed his cup of cocoa on the bench and asked, "Petee, what're talkin' about.

"I'm a jinx, Ike. You've got to stop hangin with bad luck me." Feldman shook his head in disbelief, "Don't talk like that, Petee. You know that ain't true."

"It's true, alright, Ike." A tense look filled his eyes. His voice sounded hollow, dreamy. "First it was my Mom - she got herself sick and died in that hospital. I never really knew her, Ike." Then there was the fire and we lost everything. We were real lucky to get out alive." His voice lowered more somberly, "Grandma tried hard to stay alive to take care of the bunch of us." He shrugged his shoulders and and drifted in thought.

Feldman sat closer to the agitated teen. He placed his arm around Peter's shoulders, but the distraught boy pulled away. "No, Ike!" he said when he jammed his hands into his pockets and stepped away. Turning he said, "Ike, I'm a jinx, that's all." He stormed out of the gym while his bewildered friend stood stunned by this temper.

Peter trudged through knee deep snow, arduously forcing himself forward until he arrived at the cemetery. Once inside the gate the somber boy stared down at Ralph Benson's tombstone. And then, in a flash of memory he reflected back to the impatience of his dead friend. He remembered how his own stupid remarks always brought swears gushing from Ralph. It seemed so long ago and yet, it felt it was yesterday when they visited the peanut lady.

He knelt in the unblemished snow and blessed himself, then slowly brushed the snow off the headstone. "Jeez, Ralph," he complained, how in the hell do you stand this cold.." Catching his mistake he chuckled, "Yea, like you're standing, huh, Ralph." he then quickly apologized, "And here I go again with another dumb remark." He bare handedly cleared snow off the grave itself and then sat at its foot. Suddenly, he bubbled enthusiastically, "We had King Philip's War today, Ralph." It was a spontaneous feeling of relief where his feelings of regret he showed to his friend Ike suddenly seemed unimportant. He was with his friend Ralph now and that meant so much more to him. "You would have liked the fun we had beating each other up, Ralph." he continued, "The whole school was split in half - a bunch of us was Indians and the rest was Settlers."

His enthusiasm was now building where he slid closer to the headstone and draped his arm over it. "We built huge icy snow forts that looked a mile high and we attacked. Gee, Ralph, it was lots of fun." He smiled brightly when he relived his experiences. "I even snuck into the Settlers fort and tried to steal the bags they took from us. But, they caught me and dumped me out of their fort." Wriggling uncomfortably he repositioned himself. "Us Indians lost by only five points, darn it." He ran his finger into the etched engraving of the headstone and said, "I'm still not swearing like you used to, Ralph. Instead of 'darn it' I shoulda said something like 'oh shit' That's what you woulda said huh?"

He took his hat and dusted the snow off the tombstone and asked, You came down to see King Philip's War, didn't ya, Ralph?" The boy paused, now hanging his head while in deep thought and then abruptly smiled thinly when he looked up showing a tear slipping down his cheek. He wiped it away with the back of his glove and said, "I guess I'm just a sissy." He sniffled noisily and abruptly changed the subject.

The youth dusted snow from his boots and then became very serious. "Remember my friend Bix? I........I told you about him last summer. He's the guy who wanted to join the submarines. Well, Bix....Bix got himself blinded in the navy. Now he can't see." The boy tightened his arms around his knees to give himself more warmth and continued, "Bix and me was good friends and I miss him just as much as I miss you, Ralph. Bix is a hero now cuz he tried to help some other guys taking submarine training with him. Something about an accident with steam.

Well, I'm still hangin 'round Feldman. I told you about him before, remember, Ralph? He's the kid I gave a nickname Ike to. I told you about that too? He stood up and slowly started walking toward the gate, then turned and asked, "Ralph, I got something that's bothering me. Do you mind if I ask you?" He reclaimed his seat and continued, "Well, I wonder if I'm a jinx. I mean...." he hesitated, now wrinkling his nose at what he was about to ask. "I keep thinking if it wasn't for me you'd still be alive. And....and if it wasn't for me Bix wouldn't be blind."

"You know what? It's like all my life people I get to love either die or they....they have things happen to them." He frowned down upon himself for he felt so uncomfortable talking about something that was so confusing to him. "Well, my Mom - she was put in a hospital when I was a little baby and then....and then nine years later she died in that hospital. They took me to see her about five times that I remember. But, Ralph, I didn't really know her. She was just another woman - d-ya know what I mean? I was almost afraid of her..

Nobody in my family talked about her much. I guess it was a big secret. Anytime I asked about her they all clammed up. Ya know, Ralph, I kinda figured it out myself. I figured she must have been Koo Koo, or crazy or something like that." He leaned close to the headstone and whispered, Ya know what, Ralph? I ain't never told anybody about this. You're the only person that knows, so can you kinda keep it a secret?"

Peter took a deep breath, feeling as if a great load had been shrugged away. Standing now he wrapped his arms across his chest when he walked to the gate, turned and asked, "Gees, Ralph, how can you live in this cold?"

When he left the cemetery he followed the same footsteps he had made when he arrived. It was getting dark with a full moon casting eerie shadows through the trees. His damp clothes offered little protection from the biting cold that was being pushed by a gentle breeze, chilling him all the more. Suddenly, in the distance he saw a solitary figure walking toward him. He gasped at the thought if it was an Instructor he would surely get a demerit for wandering the island without permission.

There was no turning back or even attempting to hide from whomever it was for he must certainly have seen Peter by the glow of the moon. Why else would he be getting nearer. Apprehensively now he continued toward the person, knowing full well he was doomed to that demerit. To his surprise he seemed to recognize the person the closer he came. Surely....surely - could it be? Yes! It was his friend Isaiah Feldman. Peter waved in relief when he rushed to his friend and gasped, "What are you doing way out here?" he shook his head back and forth in disbelief, "Ya know, we can both get demerits for this?"

"Yea, I know." Feldman answered quickly.

"Well, whatcha doin' here? Peter sounded exasperated.

"I followed you." came a quick reply.

Peter looked confused, "Why you following me?"

"Cuz you're my friend. I was worried about you." it was a precise answer, short and crisp.

The two teens started back to the main campus. For a few moment there was not one word between the two until Peter explained, "Well, I went to see Ralph Benson. I had something to ask him." Peter glanced sideways at his friend knowing for sure what kind of remark was next to come. Feldman suddenly stopped walking. It was obvious Feldman had just been shocked. "You speak to dead people? he asked incredulously. Peter simply hunched his shoulders, hoping he would not really have to answer the question.

Now hoping to avoid Feldman's question Peter asked quickly, "Did you really mean it when you said you was worried about me and that you're my friend? He held his breath hoping Feldman would not ask questions about Ralph Benson.

"That's why I came to find you." The two boys faced each other where they were framed by the casting moon.

"Ike, you know I'm Greek, huh?"

"Yea and I'm a Jew. So what?"

"Well, in the Greek if a man meets a man friend they kiss." The boy suddenly became uncomfortable that he even brought up the subject. "I mean...." he instantly tried to clarify his statement, "Not kissy type stuff that a guy does with a girl....I mean on the lips. They kiss each other's cheek. That's cuz they're friends. You know what I mean?"

Feldman looked down at his boots when he kicked a clump of snow. Finally he answered, "I guess a lot of nationalities do that. Even the Italians, the French and we do it too. The Jews do it too." Peter persisted with the direction he brought the conversation. "Well, that kiss ain't mushy or girly type kissin. It's man kissin. It means we're friends."

Feldman frowned in concern. "What are you talkin about, Petee?"

Peter suddenly blurted, "I'm gonna kiss you - cuz you're my friend."

Feldman's top lip wavered. His eyes bulged in surprise. "What! Are you crazy?" he looked around wide eyed. "I ain't letting you kiss me, Petee. No one will understand."

"Well I ain't crazy, Ike. You're my friend and I'm your friend and so I'm gonna kiss you like a man does to his friend. Once on each cheek."

There was a long hesitation. Feldman finally snickered, "Common, Petee. You're kidding me, ain't-cha? This is a joke, huh?" "We can just shake hands, can't we?" he asked hopefully

Peter looked offended. He answered, "That kiss makes us friends until the day we die." His eyes betrayed the challenge he was making. "You said you're my friend, Ike. Now prove it."

The boys stood in the middle of a snow covered dirt road. Feldman jammed his hands into his pockets and swayed left and right. He knew Peter was dead serious and he was very uncomfortable with what his friend asked him. "I'm your friend, Petee. No matter what.

"Well, put your hands on my shoulders and I'll do the same to you." Peter ordered.

"Jeez, Petee." Feldman offered one more plea, but it was obvious Peter was quite determined.

They stood quietly facing each other with their hands clasped on each other's shoulders. A concerned frown appeared on Isaiah's face when he starred impassively into Peter's eyes that were now focused challengingly and determined. Peter leaned forward and gently kissed his friend's left cheek and then the right one. Feldman blushed when he too kissed Peter's cheeks.

"Is it over, Petee?" A chilling, frosty mist exhaled from Feldman's mouth when he wiped his hand across his lips. "So that makes us friend's for life?" he asked hopefully.

They continued walking through the chilled night toward the main campus. Each boy was caught up in his own thoughts. Peter's mind was in a whirlwind because he had dredged up all of these memories and was only now regretting even mentioning such private matters to his friend Feldman. His eyes strayed up the long hill ahead where the main campus was coming into focus. He was glad he was living on the island for he felt he had escaped the misery of the tenement. It was not that he did not love his family, it was just that his father was living in a rut. It was as if his father had given up the struggle to pull himself out of the endless pit tenements offered. At least he gave his father credit for getting him into this school despite the fact Peter had to earn his own way in funding his tuition by going after every scholarship the school had to offer.

Feldman's voice seemed distant at first and then Peter instantly brought himself back to reality. "Petee, you went to visit Ralph Benson cuz you had something to ask him? He warmed up a questioning smile for his curiosity had now peaked. He then asked sheepishly, "Can you tell me what that's all a bout?"

Peter paused for a moment. He wondered if Isaiah would understand. Finally, he answered, "You're probly gonna think I'm nuts, Isaiah." He found it difficult to look his friend in the eyes. "I wanted to know if Ralph thought I was a jinx, that's all." Feldman frowned at the incredible answer. His brow knit into a scowl when he looked directly at Peter and blurted, "You asked him that?"

"Yea," Peter was quick to answer, I always ask him things when something's bothering me."

"And he answered you?" The boy's voice rose with anxiety. Large brown eyes were fixed questioningly.

"No Ike!" Peter defended, Ralph's dead. Now how can he speak to me?"

Peter was irritated with the questions, "It's just a feeling I get. Like....like maybe I'm talking to God through Ralph. I....I feel like I get answers." A scowl rippled across his forehead when he continued, "Don't ask me what it is. It makes me feel good, that's all." A satisfied smile crept across Feldman's face. He placed his arm around Peter's shoulders when they finally arrived at their dormitory. Before they entered Peter said, "You're a good friend Ike. There's a lot of nice guys at this school, but there aren't any who would have taken that long walk in the middle of winter, especially after he just got out of the infirmary, to come and find me." A flattered smile appeared on Feldman's lips when he answered, "Yea, thanks Petee. Now I know what you meant with that kissing the cheek stuff."

CHAPTER EIGHT

A MYSTERY SOLVED

It was the day before Peter's class was to give the assembly presentation at the evenings gathering of the entire student body. The teenager had apprehensively approached his teacher with a special request. "Mrs. Robertson?" he asked, "Do you think I can do an act that I've worked out with my friend Ike?" He held his breath for he knew changing the format of a previously selected presentation would certainly not be approved. But, what did he have to lose.

The weekly assemblies were designed so designated classrooms had a chance to make a presentation to the rest of the student body. Each presentation was to be creative and performed by each member of that particular class. This was an important part of the learning experience. And now the buxom woman smiled down at the inquiring face. She had a persistent problem adjusting her glasses, especially when she was annoyed at answers to questions that were wrong.

She peered over the tops of her glasses and asked, "We seem to have our presentation pretty well worked out, young man. Don't you think?" She frowned at the boy's upturned face. The youngster crossed his arms across his chest for he knew he would have to be very convincing, after all, you don't barge in when the program is ready and then throw a curve ball into it. Peter was getting nervous at the thought he would be ridiculed, but he was determined to be persistent. His usual role was too memorize a poem, which he was good at, but it seemed such a minor role for him.

"It's just that Isaiah and me have a funny skit that might give our class a big boost." he eyed her skeptically.

Mrs. Robertson wiped her brow with a tissue and asked, "You mean you want me to approve a skit I haven't seen? You expect me to agree to something that could be offensive.?

"Well....Well, Mrs. Robertson," he defended, "it's something I call The Zeider Zee' - and....and it's kinda funny, I think."

She studied the boy for a moment, now troubled that giving him too much liberty could do more harm than good. But, one thing she always approved was to give boys a chance at self expression. Maybe this time - even though she felt like giving in to the boy's request, she still needed more information. "Why not give me a hint of what it's all about." Peter grinned back for he knew he just got over the first hurdle.

He bubbled enthusiastically,,. Now his words flowed like water pouring down a drain pipe. "Mrs. Robertson, The Zeider Zee is a name that was given to the big wall that kept the ocean out of Holland. And.... And I have a kind sing-along and dumb dance routine about the boy who saved the population by sticking his finger in a hole that suddenly leaked water. It's about the....the...." he was so excited he suddenly went into a slow dance step of the routine while pointing his finger at an imaginary hole. He looked up at his teacher hopiing she understood.

"Now slow down, Peter." Robertson admonished, "I know you're anxious by this skit, but you haven't told me what Mister Feldman has to do with it."

Peter took a deep breath and smiled sheepishly, "Well, Ike, he plays the cymbal."

The startled woman could not believe her ears. Her voice rose in disbelief. "A cymbal!" she blurted, "Just one cymbal?" Her eyes bulged into a confused stare.

Peter realized he better not lose the momentum he had built. "Yea, Mrs. Robertson. He's kinda-like my straight man. Only I kinda pick on him."

"Oh, you kinda pick on him." she mimicked his expression. A thin smile appeared on her face. "Well, let's you and I discuss this further." She smiled down at the boy, still unconvinced whether to let this new episode conflict with what had already been prepared. For the next hour teacher and student sat huddled in the empty classroom. The boy had his hands full trying to convince the doubting educator of his skit. He outlined the entire act in detail, at the same time crossing his fingers behind his back so she would not see his nervousness. She warmed up a thin smile and said, "If I let you go on with this skit, will you promise me one thing? Peter gulped in anticipation while he waited and shaking his head in agreement.

"I want you to promise you will not embarrass me or the ninth grade class, for if you do, you will embarrass me. And if I have to answer to Headmaster Williamson...." she pushed her glasses onto the bridge of her nose and then said with finality, "If I have to answer to Headmaster Williamson then your grades will suffer." She peered over the tops of her glasses for emphasis, "You could flunk this class."

Peter gleamed a toothy smile back at her, even though he knew he was treading on dangerous grounds. But he had won! He wanted to leap up and down. He had won! He wanted to shout for joy, but he knew better than to make a fool of himself. He wanted one bit of assurance when he asked excitedly, "You mean we can do it, Mrs. Robertson?" He jumped out of his chair, tightened his fists and punched the air. "Yea!" he shouted, We'll show you, Mrs. Robertson!"

And then as an afterthought he blurted, "You won't have to answer to Moley....oops!" he caught his blunder and then corrected, "I....I mean Mister Williamson.."

Robertson glared through her glasses and asked, "Moley? Who is Moley?"

The boy stared back wide-eyed. He could just have ruined everything he worked so hard for. "Er....Er, Ma-am, I think I just goofed." He started for the door and tried awkwardly to change the subject, "Thank You, Mrs. Robertson. Thanks again, Ma-am. We'll make you real proud of us." He took a deep breath and without looking back slipped out the door leaving the wide-eyed teacher who's question went unanswered. When he slipped out the door he leaned against the wall and exhaled slowly, now wishing he could kick himself for letting such a slip pass.

That night the performance went off as scheduled. Peter and Isaiah went on with their foolish skit with one boy punching the air imitating plugging a hole in the dike while the other foolishly struck his cymbal.

They looked like two stiff penguins dancing on the ice at the North Pole. There was no laughter from the student audience. A numbing void filled the vast auditorium. Peter's heart plunged when he took a quick look at Headmaster Williamson who never cracked a smile.

It was after the performance where Peter and Isaiah sat quietly in an ante-room , subdued and miserably despondent. They could hear the student body leaving the assembly hall. The two boys looked drained. Not a word crossed between them. Suddenly, a bulky frame filled the door. Glaring eyes were fixed on the two rascals.

Pappas reacted instantly. "Jeez, Mrs. Robertson. No one laughed at our funny skit." He looked at her innocently, still staggered at the lack of response by the other students. The corpulent teacher's face remained solemn. "Headmaster Williamson has asked me to come to his office tomorrow morning." There was a dreaded silence in the room.

Peter gulped nervously for he remembered she had warned him if there was any problem with their skit their grades would suffer. She studied the two boys letting the stillness in the room deafen them. Peter took a quick look at Feldman now sitting riveted in his seat. Suddenly, it dawned on Peter he never told Ike grades would suffer If the skit failed. He held back because he knew his friend would bow out in that case. But, he was determined not to let anything interfere with the spoof . Peter pensively looked down at his shoes, "I guess your meeting's gonna be about us? Huh, Mrs. Robertson?"

"It's 'going' to be about you, young man." she corrected. He squirmed in his seat and said, "I guess I get an 'F' for this course?" Before she answered he remembered Feldman might flunk too. "That doesn't mean Ike's gonna flunk, does it ma-am?" he asked with any luck .

She suddenly snapped, "When will you boys learn that in the nineth grade we use correct grammar?" She had not told the boys that meeting with the Headmaster was related to the curriculum and had nothing to do with the failed act. But, the boys needed a lesson. "Yes, there's a possibility Mister Feldman might flunk too." She hid a quick smile and then continued, "Tomorrow I want you both in class one half hour early." She turned and left abruptly.

Peter tried with all of his might to make sense as to why not one his own classmates even snickered at his skit. Earlier, when he tossed the ideas to some of them they encouraged him. They were behind him. Feldman just hunched his shoulders in a gesture of giving up.

The two boys hurried out of the building. Peter was strangely quiet when Isaiah said, "You ain't gonna let Mrs. Robertson get you shook up, are you? Peter ignored the question when they arrived at their dormitory for the conversation was dismissed for the moment.

Once they arrived on their floor the two boys were quickly surrounded by their fellow dormitory mates. Peter stood wide-eyed. He gulped deeply expecting the other teens to ridicule them. Cheers erupted by his mates. "You guys did great!" some called. Others slapped them on the back and languished them with praise. Peter, looking stunned asked, "But why didn't you guys laugh?" he asked incredulously. "It was the big guys. Someone explained. "They told us if we laughed we'd get punched out." Another voice cut through the din, "We did what they said or else, Petee." he doubled his fist in a gesture of being beaten.

Peter smiled over at Feldman who was leaning against a wall with arms folded and relief on his face. In that moment Peter frowned in anger when Feldman smiled knowingly at the trick the senior students had pulled on them. Peter's glare softened when the thought of what was a typical joke in a school like this came rushing home.

On the next day the problems with Mrs. Robertson had been cleared up. She understood fully the circumstances which led to the fiasco of the previous evening's assembly program. Peter and Isaiah rushed to their dormitory get rid of text books for it was their free time. Band practice had been called off so it gave the two boys time to play in the gym.

Once in their room, Peter found a note laying on his bed. When the boy picked up the note he said, "Jeez, I hope this ain't something to screw up our gym time.." He sprawled himself on the bed and read the note. Suddenly, his face turned ashen. He turned frozen, unblinking eyes at the questioning Isaiah when he handed the note to his friend and lay back with is head propped under his arms waiting for Ike's reaction. Feldman read the note aloud:

"To the two queers. I saw yous guys kissin. You're
gonna have to pay me to keep my mouth shut or im
gonna tell all the other guys about you two fayries.
I'll be in tuch later. Yous too fagots."

The offensive note with its spelling mistakes went unsigned. Isaiah sat on Peter's bed despondently as he continued to study the note. His face was pinched in a frown when he tossed the offensive note to Petee who seached through it again. Pappas leaned forward with a blank glare firmly fixed in his eyes. He shot up from his bed and waved the incriminating note like a flag. "We're gonna get this guy, Ike!" he shouted through a controlled snarl.

Isaiah clasped his hands to his head. A slight trembling of his lips soon turned into a masked quivering smile when he added, "This blackmailing son-of-a-bitch is asking to get his head punched in." A sweet venomous smile met Peter's questioning stare. "That's the first time I ever heard you swear, Ike." he smiled mischievously at his friend's sudden outburst.

Isaiah suddenly felt a searing release of the tension which built up so suddenly. He grasped a pillow and bashed it with a closed fist, "and he's gonna get this!" He smacked the pillow again and again, "Yea, Petee and I ain't gonna stop "till he bleeds all over himself. And yea, I do have a temper! And yea, I do know swears."

He looked down at his shoes and dropped his voice close to a whisper, "someplace inside me." He jerked his head up and stared at his friend, now looking perplexed, however, the puzzle was gnawing at him when he finally said, "Petee, there was nobody around. Everyone was in the gym celebrating.

Peter was deeply offended with the note's content. Still trying to put the pieces together he found it almost hopeless since the celebrating King Philip's War continued in the gym. "You know, Ike," he swung his legs so he faced his friend, "if any of the guys from the gym left they would probably go to their dorm to get out of their wet clothes. Someone never got to the gym, either they were working or they were...." his eyes licked at Feldman, "....or they were sick in the infirmary."

Feldman leaped on the concept when he added, "And from the infirmary you can see all the way down the south end, especially if you...." he suddenly fixed a toothy smile at Peter, "....if you've got a pair of binoculars." he sucked in his breath with his anxiety. Peter was not about to let this opportunity slip passed when he asked excitedly. "And who's the only kid in this school that's got binoculars?

"MACDOUGAL!" the two voices blended in unison.

"And who's been in the infirmary all week?" a sly smile graced Peter's lips.

"MacDougal!" Feldman answered as he leaped for joy when he pranced around the room, his hands in fists while punching the air in a make believe boxing match.

Peter scooted back to his bed, laying down so he studied the ceiling. His mind raced trying to find a solution how to expose the culprit. Suddenly he reached over and grasped Ike's hand in a vice-like grip. His friend applied pressure to his friends hand equally. In that instant the two boys tumbled on the floor now wrestling each other aggressively.

"And I'm gonna punch MacDougal's freckled face until he begs for mercy." Peter shrieked with laughter when he punched his friend's shoulder lightly.

"And I'm gonna choke him like this." Feldman grinned demonically when he straddled his friend, barring his teeth menacingly he cupped his hands around Peter's throat gently.

Their excited voices filled the dormitory room with nonsensical laughter when the boys wrestled more enthusiastically. Suddenly, the door opened when Mister. Clifton's frame filled the opening. He peered down over the tops of his glasses at the two miscreants who had instantly stopped their silliness. Two pairs of eyes looked up, now focused on those of the instructor. Gulping nervously the boys broke apart only to sit squarely in the middle of the floor almost, but not quite, defiantly.

Mr. Clifton finally broke the silence, "I hope you two are not serious. You're not fighting, are you?" He crossed his arms and waited for a response.

"Oh nooo, Mr. Clifton." Peter chuckled when he scrambled to his feet. "We ain't fight'n. We was just wrestling." He looked down at Feldman, "Huh, Ike. Tell Mister Clifton we was wrestling, that's all."

The adult closed the door behind him when he entered and sat on the edge of Peter's bed. He waited for an explanation. It was then that the two boys took the adult into their confidence and explained to him about the suspicion of MacDougal's threat of exposing their friendly kiss and possibly spreading a rumor around the school. Feldman handed him the obnoxious note and explained how they were going to bring the matter to MacDougal and force a confession out of him.

The Instructor read the note carefully, then inserted it into his shirt pocket. The room became very quiet while the adult thought things out. Finally, he said, "You're not to do anything with MacDougal. You're going to leave this matter with me and I'll get to the bottom of this."

Petee was not going to let things drop without an explanation. He defended his actions with the kiss when he explained, "It's not the way it looks." He was afraid the whole incident would be looked at in the wrong light. It was up to him to prove the event was trivial, it was unimportant. "I told Ike that in my nationality men kiss each other's cheek when they meet. It's....It's a sign of respect, sir."

The instructor toyed with the offensive note, "What you've just admitted is nothing new. Many men in other nationalities do the same thing." he let the matter drop and nodded in agreement. "It's quite possible MacDougal really is the culprit behind the note. Don't get involved. I'll look into it further."

He abruptly left the room. The two boys stood silently, now eyeing each other that they had scored a victory.

CHAPTER NINE

NEW ADVENTURES

Edward Winter, the noted historian, arrived on the island for his annual visit. He was well like because his stories of storm tosses seas that sank clipper ships along the New England coast captivated his young audience. He spoke of heroic exploits by valiant seamen who dared battle pirates about armed brigantines where many of the cutthroats met their death swaying from a ship's yardarm.

There were stories of vast hoards of hidden treasure, supposedly buried where ancient maps often led searchers astray. And then, tales of specters, phantoms and ghosts seen on islands close to Thompson's raised the hackles of youthful necks. Chilling epics of murder, torture and executions committed by blue uniformed soldiers upon gray clad infantrymen - doomed men captured after bloody battles on Southern lands with strange names. And then, there were ghostly ladies-in-black, haunting forts while searching in vain for their condemned mates. Edward Winter had taken a small group of students to the tip of the north end were he taught them to scale flat rocks along the tops of waves. The purpose was to see how many times the rocks would bounce before sinking. He always challenged what he called, "the achievers" - youths who would at least try to outperform one another. Winters was a master teacher.

The boys scurried to find flat stones, then skipped them over the water. Many failed and the stones simply sank. Peter paid particular attention to the trick Winter's used and in due time he managed the skill at unerringly skipping stones. When following the historian he saw him try to remove a small white stone from the edge of an embankment. The stone did not budge. Undaunted, he dug his finger along the stone's edge and removed years of encrusted soil. Seeing Peter observing him he called the boy over and asked, "Do you see anything peculiar about this stone? The fifteen year old poked his finger along the same unearthed edge and said, "It's just a little stone as far as I can see, sir."

A simple smile appeared on the adult's face when he advised, "Dig a little deeper, young man and we'll see where it leads us."

Peter's finger stabbed at the ground, loosening more soil while exposing an elongated tube-like substance, hard and unyielding. "It looks like a bone of some kind, sir." The boy's enthusiasm escalated. By now the other boys circled the pair, watching curiously.

In moments jackknives were offered as tools, making the effort easier.

Now following the shape of the extended substance Peter suddenly shouted, "There's a foot here. Look at the toes." He gaped at Mister Winter when he pointed more emphatically, "There's a leg of a dead guy or something." Winter ordered another youngster to fetch a shovel and said, "It looks like we've uncovered a mystery on Thompson's Island."

Headmaster Williamson, Coach Johnson and Mister Clifton arrived after being summoned. Digging painstakingly slowed since it would not do to disturb human bones. Peter relieved another student since more shovels had arrived. He dug carefully to the right of the bared skeleton when suddenly he shouted, "Mister Winter, Sir. I've found another skeleton." The boy looked up in amazement at the find.

Pappas meticulously moved shards of moldy coffins and then a skull appeared where hollow eye sockets stared back at the eager student. Peter held the skull high in the air and impishly exclaimed, "He needs to see a dentist real bad."

Winter glowered at the comedic youth. "Show some respect for the dead, young man. What we have here is...." A shout from the other side of the second skeleton interrupted him. "Here's another one!" The historian quickly raced over. From his left another boy yelled, "We've found a fourth one." The pulse of excitement filled the area. Now the four adults closely studied the grisly find.

Two detectives arrived with the police boat which was docked at the pier. The boys were taken off the dig when the remains were scrutinized more closely by the officials. "They don't look like they've been murdered," A detective announced. "I don't see any punctures or bullet holes." He hesitated for a moment when he took another look and said, "Unless....unless they were poisoned.

Now the dig took on a more disciplined, more archeological type of exposure for Mister Winter knew from past experience that crucial evidence could be lost when amateurs got involved. Plans were made that the bones were to be taken to a laboratory in Boston for analysis. The school buzzed with excitement, however, all of the students were now kept away.

The next day the headlines of the local newspapers blared: "FOUR FOUND BURIED ON THOMPSON'S ISLAND," while another banner read: "MYSTERY OF FOUR SKELETONS FOUND AT BOY'S SCHOOL." Boat loads of reporters, police investigators and archeologists swarmed the open pits. After a day of discovery some of the bones were sent to Harvard's Pathological Department for further analysis.

The next day Peter's assignment was to rake the oval cinder track around the football field which brought him close to the activity at the North End. Suddenly a heavy set reporter approached the young teen. Slipping off his straw hat he wiped his brow and finally asked, "Tell me, son, what do you think about all this dead body stuff?"

Peter grinned, "I helped find them, sir." he bragged

"You did? the reporter sparked to life, "You mean you actually found them?"

"Oh, no, sir." the boy corrected, "Mister Winter found them. I only helped dig them up."

"Well, young feller, let me take your picture." He stepped back and posed Peter so the background was filled with investigators in the distance.

"What's your name, son and how old are you?"

"I'm Peter Pappas." he answered proudly. "I'm fifteen, sir.' The next day a headline appeared in only one newspaper:

FIFTEEN YEAR OLD FINDS SKELETONS ON ISLAND." The accompanying article read:

BOSTON AMERICAN - Fifteen year old Peter Pappas, a student at the boy's school on Thompson's Island gets credit for discovering unidentified remains of four skeletons at the island school. Peter, a sophomore, described in detail the finding of a knee bone which led to the discovery. This brings some doubt as to the claim by renowned historian Edward Winter who said he was the original discoverer. Mr. Winter argued vehemently and said the charge was preposterous and being blown out of proportion.

Winter's, a distinguished historian, who holds professorships at Harvard University and Boston University states he cannot understand why this youngster would concoct such a story. It only remains to be proven whether the noted historian is fabricating his role or whether the student is only seeking attention.

The note received by Peter Pappas was brief and cryptically written. It simply noted, "SEE ME!" and initialed by the Headmaster. The boy hesitatingly tapped on the closed door, then entered to find the portly administrator speaking on the telephone. An opened newspaper filled the top of the desk. The teenager was waved in and stood directly in front of the desk. He could not help overhearing the the conversation when Williamson said, "Yes, Mister Winter, I've read the article and am investigating it right now." Stubby fingers held a red pencil which he used to circle a section of the newspaper. "I'm sorry this has happened too." he continued, "But, let me get back to you once I've looked into the matter."

When the telephone was placed in its cradle Headmaster Williamson sat back into his chair, a creak filled the room. Peter's heart raced for he was sure he had gotten himself into some kind of trouble, for what other reason would he be called to the Headrmaster's office. He searched his memory, but for the life of him he could not recall anything he might have done.

Any of his friends that got called to the office were often on the receiving end of punishment. He took a deep breath exhaled slowly. The suspense was gripping when he shifted from one foot to the other. Finally, Mister Williamson looked stone-faced when he asked, "Young man do you read the newspapers?" The adult pursed his lips when waiting for an answer.

Peter gulped. His voice sounded hollow in the large office. "No sir." he answered, but then he brightened and continued, "But I do read magazines, Sir."

The serious overseer then asked, "Did you ever speak to a reporter about the skeletons at the North End?"

The boy smiled when the memory came back. "Oh, yes sir. A reporter took my picture." He twisted his fingers where his arms were pulled rigidly behind him.

Thickset eyebrows lifted, "And did this reporter ask you questions about finding the skeletons?"

"Oh, yes sir." And I told him I helped dig them up." A response from the administrator was a slow clearing of the adult's throat. He pointed to a chair to the left of his desk and told the boy to sit in it. He then leaned forward, a grim look was etched on his face, then he deliberately accented certain words when he spoke, "Did YOU tell this reporter that YOU alone discovered the skeletons?"

The boy squirmed in his seat. He nervously rubbed the back of his right ankle against the left ankle of the other foot and took a quick glance out the window where a crow cawed noisily from outside. "That crow's laughing at me." he thought to himself. Peter now shot a curious look into the firm gaze aimed him and then answered quickly, "No sir. I never told him nothing like that. I just told him that I helped. That Mister Winter...." He was cut off when the next pointed question was asked, "Did you in any way tell this reporter that Mister Winter DID NOT find the skeletons?"

The fifteen year old looked surprised. He eyed his mentor with a wide unblinking stare. So this is what it's about, he thought to himself. The reporter did something wrong and Peter was going to be blamed for it. Headmaster Williamson thrust the newspaper at the bewildered youth, "I want you to read what I've circled in red." Peter's hand shook slightly with nervousness and read the article. His lips moved as he read to himself. Slowly, the message registered in his mind. He let the newspaper fall on his lap, started to speak, then frowned down at himself. A feeling of helplessness overcame him.

Here he was only a teenager facing a grown-up problem that he knew would probably go against him. From past experience, which reached all the way back to before he came to this school, he often gave up defending himself because adults seldom believed him. His face flushed as anger gripped when the Headmaster's voice brought him back from his thoughts.

"This reporter tells a different story, DOESNT HE, Mister Pappas? His inquisitor pinched his lips resolutely as he waited for an answer.

The boy grimaced anxiously. He swallowed hard and without saying a word nodded his head affirmatively.

"Do you AGREE with what the reporter had to say, YOUNG MAN?" Williamson sat back into his creaky chair and waited patiently for an answer.

Suddenly Peter's brow knit into a contemptuous frown. He stood up abruptly. The accusing newspaper fell to the floor. "NO SIR!" his voice rose in anger. "NO SIR! IT'S A LIE!" I never told him anything like that." He breathed heavily when a snivel escaped from his lips. His hands trembled when he reached for the spilled newspaper and awkwardly tried to put the pages back together.

Williamson pushed forward. His voice softened when he asked the bewildered boy to sit. "Pappas, I believe you." The beefy faced Headmaster smiled tight-lipped. He was studying the boy's reaction for he was secretly pleased with the youngsters answers.

Peter was spellbound. Did he hear correctly, he thought. His tightened stomach muscles relaxed. A quick, uneasy smilled filled the youth's face. "You do believe me, sir?" he asked excitedly when he exhaled in a gasp.

The portly Headmaster did not repeat himself when he said, "Mister Pappas, this is a good lesson for you, "There are some people in this world who will do anything to succeed. In your case this reporter took advantage of the things you were trying to tell him. He twisted the story to raise doubts in the minds of his readers that one of the greatest historians of our time was lying."

The large man shifted in his seat and continued, "Maybe you've learned a lesson in all of this." His brown eyes sparkled behind thick eyeglasses. "You have nothing to worry about." he assured. "I will speak with Mister Winter and I will also speak with the editor of this....this...." he looked at the newspaper Peter had retrieved, "....so called newspaper." He shook his head in agreement and then dismissed the boy.

It was some weeks later when Peter Pappas sat in his nineth grade class where his teacher, Mrs. Robertson, had completed the history lesson. She was popular with her students because she often deviated from the lesson at hand and often introduced the boys to bits of knowledge outside the strict regimen of lesson plans. There was one time when her students were taught how archeologists structured a dig. How the search for treasures uncovered tombs of ancient kings and queens.

There was one deviation into the lifestyles of pirates who plundered and looted sailing ships on the high seas. Today, she brought up the subject of the skeletons found at the North End of the island. The history books were closed and set aside. "You all have had a month as to how those skeletons got buried on the island?"

A boy from the back of the room instantly raised his hand. "I think someone buried them, ma-am." The class burst into laughter.

"I think one of the men killed the others, then killed himself and buried his own body." Another jokester added.

"I think....." before the third boy added to the silliness Mrs.

Robinson interrupted. "I want to thank you for your in-put, young men," she went along with the juveniles rather than scold them, of course, this is what made her a unique educator. "That's not quite what I meant," she continued, now let's be more sincere and try to come with a sensible answer."

"I think they might have been escaped prisoners from the Civil War, cuz some of the prisoners were kept on island in Boston Harbor." Peter answered.

The teacher nodded in agreement, "That's a good answer. Now someone else, please."

"I think they were....maybe pirates?" Feldman held his breath in hopes his answer would be accepted.

"It's a possibility." Robinson answered, "Now let me ask you this, What if they were Indians?" The boys looked up in awe.

All eyes were fixed on the schoolteacher when a hand shot from the left side of the room. "Ma-am, I ain't never heard of Indians living on islands.

She smiled at the statement, "Now that makes it a mystery, doesn't it? It seems that t Harvard University they analyzed the bones and have determined the skeletons are those of Indians. Now, Roger, you said you never heard of Indians living on islands and you are right." A murmur filled the room when the story started to get exciting.

Peter," she asked, "You helped uncover the skeletons. Did you see any beads or hatchets, headbands or feathers or anything that might prove they were actually Indians?"

"No, Ma-am, there was nothing like that." he answered quickly, "Just rotten caskets."

Mrs. Robinson leaned against her desk and crossed her arms. She was about to surprise the students and she savored the moment. "Indians had a fear of islands because they thought if they died on one their souls would not be released. If you remember from the movies you've seen Indians were always buried above ground." Not one boy moved in his seat as they were completely spellbound. "And if Indians were buried above ground how did these four get buried under the ground? Why were they encased in caskets if they were afraid their souls would not be released? Now why were they on an Island?" She waited for the message to be absorbed.

Peter raised his hand and asked, "Ma-am, what if they were not Indians and Harvard made a mistake? What if they were real people?"

"Real people?" she caught his blunder and pursued it. What do you mean real people? Aren't Indians real people?"

The boy flushed with embarrassment, "I didn't mean that, Mrs. Robinson. I meant, what if they were....I mean....oh shucks, Ma-am, you know what I mean?" He shrunk down in his seat knowing the giggles he heard from the other boys would mean they would tease him about his slip-up.

The teacher ignored the statement and then announced in a clear, voice, "Missionaries!" An outburst of excited voices filled the room. "Yes, missionaries. What if a group of missionaries lived on Thompson's Island and the Indians were converted to Christianity?"

"Gosh, Mrs. Robinson," Isaiah asked, "then that would account for the wooden caskets, huh?"

At that moment a clattering bell signaled classes were over. The schoolroom emptied quickly. Petee and Isaiah rushed to their dormitory room to change clothes and take advantage of free time. Peter advised his friend he had an errand to do and that meant they would meet later and play some basketball in the gym. He pulled on his winter coat and rushed from the dormitory. Once outdoors he slowed his pace for he did not want to call attention to himself.

He smiled with anxiety when he approached a side door to the huge Bulfinch building. Taking a furtive look to see if he was being watched he slipped behind the door and entered what used to be an old bakery - a holdover from the days before the new dining room was built. It was of no use these days except as a short-cut into the administrative section of the building.

Huge, empty ovens were now covered with dust. A dank smell filled the room for the windows were never opened any more. The boy positioned himself where he was half hidden behind one of the ovens and waited anxiously, shifting his weight from one foot to the other.

The room was deathly still, yet the sound of activity filtered through the closed door leading to the offices. He hoped his plan would work, however, with time passing quickly he almost abandoned his idea.

Finally, he heard the inner door open and quick steps scuffed along the cement floor. Peter's heart skipped a beat when the Headmasters daughter, Sheryl-Ann, had stopped by to see her father, the Headmaster and was now on her way home by using the bakery short-cut. Peter knew her timetable very well for he had watched her from afar when his job took him to the office to pick up mail after school. His nervousness sent a shudder of exhilaration through every membrane in his system. He knew he had only one chance to make his move and he hoped his courage would not fail him.

Stepping from behind the oven he innocently greeted the startled girl who recognized him as her classmate who tossed off a few harmless remarks about his bumping into her. The boy trembled when he approached, for his eyes were fixed on the sparkle in her green eyes. He smiled back sheepishly and then suddenly blurted, "Sheryl-Ann, can....can," he stuttered, "can I kiss you?" He gulped nervously for it was an instant of pure fear that gripped him - it was unthinkable to back away.

She smiled brightly at the oncoming youth and then without hesitation simply answered, "Sure, Petee, why not?" Peter stopped his forward progress when he was overwhelmed by the quick, unexpected, response. He expected to be rejected, perhaps even scorned by the pretty girl. In the same instant he wondered what would happen if she, God forbid, told her father.

His mouth felt very dry when he approached slowly for it would not do to rush and force her to change her mind. His mind swirled with questions, "Will he hold her in his arms like they do in the movies, or is it best not to touch her at all? Was he going to be clumsy? He never kissed a girl on the lips before and what on earth was he going to do with his eyes?

He was now standing in front of her for the girl dropped her textbooks where they fell noisily to the floor. She had tilted her head back and closed her eyes, waiting expectantly. Peter concentrated on her face where he now focused on her pursed lips. A shy, uncertain smile filled his face when he gently touched his lips to hers.

He was instantly overwhelmed when the soft lips blended with his obsession. The spell enveloped him with pulsating signals, spiraling like a whirlwind through every inch of his body. His legs suddenly weakened for his mind spun like a top making him dizzy enough to feel like he would slump to the floor.

It was as if an eternity had passed when she finally parted. He smiled shyly at the grinning girl and it was here he finally found the words to say, "Gee, thanks, Sheryl-Ann." He knew it was a clumsy thing to say, but with all the new emotions that ripped through him he could find nothing else to say.

She scooped up her books from the floor and wheeled away while shaking her hair so her dark brown tresses would fall into place. With the boy staring wide-eyed after her she waved her hand and in a sing-song voice that echoed in the empty chamber she flippantly said, "Byee, Byee, Petee."

Peter, now numbed by the experience sat on a bench in the dark bakery. He thrust trembling hands under his armpits, then shut his eyes, smiled to himself and said aloud, "Oh yea! Was that ever nice!"

CHAPTER TEN

SAINT PAUL'S

It was spring of 1945 when a challenge by arch rival Saint Paul's Catholic Memorial brought the entire student body to the baseball field. The day was hot and dry that summer's day. An east wind blew gently, drifting ominously from neighboring Spectacle Island. A fair east wind meant the stench from Boston's garbage now housed on Spectacle Island where it was processed as fertilizer. It was not a situation that happened every day, but when it did it was overwhelming - an undefiled airiness that was beyond anyone's control.

From the dock the Pilgrim's horn blew shrilly, announcing the arrival of the competitors from the Saint Paul's school. Peter dressed in a baseball uniform sat quietly on a bench now that practice was over. The diamond was left for the opposing team warm-ups. Pappas squirreled his nose at the offensive smell from Spectacle Island. A boy seated next to Peter said, I bet the Saint Paul's guys will have a field day nick-naming us with that garbage stink.."

Peter nodded in agreement when the youngster next to him continued, "A lot of people think we're in jail out here on the island. They think we're a bunch of juvenile delinquents. Ya know what, Petee," his enthusiasm quickly developed with his story, "When Coach ran the boat one day he took me along as his boat boy and when we arrived at City Point a bunch of kids asked me why I got put away."

Peter had an idea what the boy was about to say and seemed nonplussed about hearing some lie. "I said my mother was starving and I stole a loaf of bread, but I got caught and was sent to the island instead of jail." He smiled to himself when he relived the memory. Peter was upset with what he heard and snapped, "Jeez, that was a lousy thing to say. What the hell's the matter with you, Sully?" The boy simply shrugged his shoulders and giggled when he walked away from any more criticisms.

The baseball field suddenly filled with the opposing team taking practice, a pre-game option to limber up before the game. Peter eyed each player critically, analyzing their strengths. He watched the Saint Paul's pitcher who snapped a unique curve ball which came in close to the batter then arched away when it flew over the plate. But, the mistake he observed was the pitcher gave his throw away when he dried his hand on his pant leg before he threw the curve.

Pappas smiled to himself for he could now anticipate the pitch by stepping into it when it reached the plate. He would delay his swing and smack the ball into right field which could possibly give him exta bases. His friend Isaiah stood off to the side swinging a bat to limber up. A quick thumbs-up passed between the two boys who worked as playing buddies because they were such close friends and could anticipate each others playing habits.

The game began. Saint Paul's players quickly antagonized the Thompson boys with their taunts. The foul smells from Spectacle Island continued to cloud the island despite it being a bright sunny day. Peter reached second base after he hit a single between the third baseman and the shortstop. The charging outfielder overplayed the ball, letting it go past him for an extra base to second. The opposing second baseman crowded close to Peter and snapped, "You were lucky on that one, shit schooler."

Peter's neck hairs prickled at the insult, but gave his antagonist a quick smirk, "Wait 'till I get up to bat again, Pope's boy." He was ready with an answer to any caustic remark that came his way. From home plate a crack of the bat sent Peter racing to third base when the ball fell between the center and right fielder. He was in scoring postion where cheers from the bleachers filled the air. Mister Clifton's voice cut through the cheers, encouraging him to score.

"Yer out!" the home base umpire yelled when a Thompson batter missed the ball for the third strike.

With two outs Peter's attention quickly turned back to the game. He mentally measured the long distance between third base and home plate. Knowing the burly catcher crowded the base when someone raced home presented a new problem for him. The tension was building for there were now two outs which gave the Thompson team only one hope for a score. Suddenly, a bat met the pitched ball that skittered along the first baseline. The defensive first baseman and the pitcher clumsily chased the ball which gave Peter the one chance to fly home and score.

As he raced home his eyes were focused the heavy-set Saint Paul's catcher who loomed like a giant over the plate. From the corner of his eye he could see the ball speeding for the glove of the burly catcher. Peter was now only a few feet away when he dropped to the ground letting the momentum slide perilously close to the huge adversary guarding the plate. His momentum caused him to slide perilously close to home base and at that moment he heard the ball smack into the catcher's mitt.

The dust swirled when the catcher turned and blocked the plate with his padded knee exposing only the back side of the plate. Peter slid past home plate then swung his left leg backward where his cleated shoe touched the base. The momentum of the husky catcher trying to tag the runner caused him to lose his balance and tumble on top of the prostrated runner. The two protagonists were now face-to-face on the ground. A sinister sneer filled the Sant Paul's humiliated catcher when he snapped, "Are you the Jew boy?" Peter trying to untangle himself from the weight of his antagonist retaliated, "Ask Jesus, you hypocrite!" At that moment the umpire yelled, "SAFE!"

Cheered by his teammates as the inning ended. Peter, covered second base as the game progressed. After two outs the burly catcher came to bat. The first pitch whizzed by in a strike. With the second pitch the batter swung and connected solidly. The sharp crack of the bat echoed it was going for extra bases. The ball arched far into center field.

The hulking brute circled first base and came charging toward second base. Peter's attention was focused on the outfielder who threw a heave which sliced the air with precision, meeting Peter's glove before

123

meeting the threat coming from first base. He turned to tag the runner who was now sliding into second base with his cleated shoes aimed dangerously high, a trick to put the defensive second baseman in a threat so he would not tag Saint Paul's catcher out.

Pivoting on one heel, Peter stubbornly braced himself with what was going to be an obvious clash of wills. The boy whirled and dropped to his left knee in hopes he could avoid the menacing cleats. If his plan worked the cleats would miss him and with the strength of his own body the two body's would glance off each other and the tag would be made.

A crush of flesh meeting flesh filled the diamond. The crowd looked stunned. All eyes wre fixed on the entanglement at second base. An eerie hush filled the air. Peter lay sprawled where the momentum deposited him a yard away from the base. The aggressive catcher lay where he had stopped his forward drive. Slowly, Peter struggled to his feet with the ball still clutched in his gloved hand. He looked down on the prostrated catcher who was knocked unconscious from the clash. A furtive smile formed on his lips when the two coaches worked on the prostrated brute.

Minutes passed when the Saint Paul's player suddenly revived. He was helped from the field where he sat droopily on the bench. The opponents coach called to the umpire, "O'Connel is out of the game. Substituting is Billy Cahane." The game progress through the full nine innings without further incident. Cheers filled the air when Thompson defeated Saint Paul's seven to three. Peter savored the victory. He limped to the bench for his leg had been bruised by the collision. Once seated Feldman sat next to him and said, "You're really a brute." he teased. Peter nodded his head and smiled.

That night the entire student body gathered by the flagpole which stood between two of the four dormitories. Members of the band played march themes from various colleges. Peter sat at the periphery of the crowd. It was here Feldman found him absorbed with the shenanigans of his schoolmates.

"Two bits Saint Paul's will come back looking for vengeance this football season." Peter's friend clapped him on the shoulder when he sat next to him.

"Oh, yea," Peter answered, "and two bits we beat them in football too."

Feldman tucked his legs under himself, now sitting Indian style, "That Saint Paul's catcher was a real s.o.b., wasn't he, Petee?" He wiped his glasses with his shirt tail and looked over at the boys by the flagpole.

Peter's expression suddenly faded to seriousness, "It was more than that." he answered grimly. The fifteen year old tucked his knees under his chin and continued, "Remember when I crashed into him at home plate, Ike?"

Yea, that's when you taught him a lesson about blocking the plate."

"Well, it was more than that. When he was on top of me he asked if I was the Jew boy."

Feldman untangled his legs. He stretched himself on the ground and propped his head into his hands, now looking at the stars showing brightly in the dark sky, "It's the same old story, isn't it?, Petee?" he asked. "It never stops no matter where we go." His voice was solemn where his eyes were still fixed on the stars.

"You know what I told him?" Peter's face hardened as he lay facing his friend, "I told him to ask Jesus. And then I called him a hypocrite."

Feldman smiled at the quick retort, "So that's why he came after you at second base.

"Yea," Peter smiled slyly, "But look what happened to him."

After a long awkward pause Feldman finally said, "You know Petee, my father was a nice guy. He taught me to be fair with other people. To be considerate of their feelings. He said I should never point a finger at someone because his color was different or his origin was not the same as mine. He used to have a small variety store in a tenement section of Boston. He often said, "We've got to take care of each other, especially during this depression. Especially now when people can't even buy a loaf of bread.' His Hebrew accent was often hard to understand, but we got by. I guess I was getting too Americanized and he didn't care."

A cynical smile appeared on Feldman's face, "We used to live over the store in a tiny apartment and always had food on the table. And that's why I think they killed him." The statement dropped like a hammer.

"They killed him!" Peter sat up in astonishment. Isaiah continued, "He used to keep a little green covered book with names of people who couldn't pay for things that they bought. Petee, there were lots of times I'd see him draw a pencil line through someone's name and he'd forget the bill. Once I saw him tear out a whole page and throw it away.

"But you said they killed him!" Peter was astonished.

"Yea, they killed him. It was done by the sons of those people he gave credit to. He was killed by those he gave free bread to. He was killed because they thought he had money." Feldman paused and then continued, "I think he was killed because he was a Jew."

Peter's temper flared, "Ike, that's awful."

Feldman hunched his shoulders. He looked over at his fellow schoolmates jostling each other near the flagpole, "It's nothing new, Petee." he continued, "I even get little digs from some of the kids around here." He smiled contemptuously.

"Here? At the school?" Peter gushed in surprise. In the four years he spent on the island he never once gave any thought that students would be so bigoted. He looked stunned and bewildered when Feldman said, "Petee, it's something you'll never understand." He was sorry he brought the subject up. Peter was his friend. He was untainted by the hostility of the others. Maybe today on the baseball diamond he might have learned that lesson.

But Feldman had one more thing to say to his naive friend. "Petee, that's being called 'prejudiced'. You see how they treat the negroes, don't you? It's....It's making judgments against someone's race even though you don't know noting about that race. My father told me that." Peter looked puzzled, for he too was searching his own mind when certain events happened in his own life.

"You still don't know - do you, Petee?" He flashed a gentle understanding smile at his friend.

"I....I think so, Ike." He tried to work out his own problem and try to relate it to what his friend told him. "When my mother was taken from us because she was....she was...." he groped for words that were sticking in his throat, "because she was insa....insane," he finally blurted it out, "people used to act kinda funny. They whispered behind our backs. It was like they were pointing their finger at us - well you know, Ike - as if we weren't like any of them. My twin sister Anna and me had a mother that was....well, you know, my mom was sick and the old Greek ladies would shake their heads and whisper to each other."

"What did they expect from us, Ike. Were we supposed to break windows? Or....or....iron clothes until they burnt to a crisp. Were we supposed to scream out the window at ghosts only she could see? It was scary, Ike, when my poor grandmother would cry seeing her only daughter in this kinda ....stress." A glimmer of a tear slipped from his eyes, "Is that this prejudice stuff you're talking about, Ike?"

Before his friend could answer, Coaches voice called out to them. "Hey you guys. Are you gonna sit there like a couple of bumps on a log." He peered ove the heads of the other students and grinned in the direction of the two friends. "Get over here and join up with the rest of the gang."

CHAPTER ELEVEN

LESSONS LEARNED

The next day, Sunday, turned brilliantly sunny. At breakfast Miss Pederson had entered with the rest of the staff. Ordinarily she would take her own meals at the farm house, but today there was a staff meeting. Most of the boys were off their work schedules where many spent their free time walking the beach or finishing personal projects.

Breakfast ended without any announcements. Peter planned his day to include a much needed talk with Miss Pederson. He stopped her before she left the dining room and plans were made for him to come to the old farm house later that afternoon. He decided to spend the few hours before his meeting with the botanist by doing some fishing from the dock. Feldman's mother arrived for an unusual meeting with her son and the Headmaster.

He arrived at the dock and cast his fishing line over the railing, now purposely distancing himself from the other boys because he wanted to sort the nagging questions he had to ask Miss Pederson. His fishing line stretched into deep water where a cork bobber floated with the pulsing waves. With the bobber in place he could tell if he had snagged a fish when the bobber suddenly disappeared. He called it "lazy-man's fishing".

The harbor waters were gently frothing, streaking toward the shore much like horses racing toward the shorline. Distant sailboats flowed with the current where their sails puffed from behind by a swelling breeze. Rolling waves lapped at the pilings holding up the wharf then split toward the beach. White seagulls soared perilously close to the pier for their instincts told them fish were being caught which meant scavaging lay ahead. Howls from student fishermen catching prized mackarel meant a hardy breakfast would be included with their meal the next morning.

A young black student passed behind Peter, then snuck behind the unsuspecting fisherman and jabbed him in the ribs with his elbow. Peter reacted by twisting toward his protagonist only to lose his fishing line where it fell into the water and snagged on a piling. "Jeez, Franklin!" he groaned while looking down at the sinewy fishing line twisted around the wooden structure. Franklin stepped back in surprise, if anything, he did not want to create a problem and yet in one motion he did just that.

The youngster looked into the water and suddenly said, "It got itself caught on a piling. That fishing line's going nowhere." A broad grin appeared on his face for now mischievous eyes flicked that an idea had crossed his mind. "Im climbing down to get that line unhooked for ya Petee." he boasted. In one motion he straddled the railing and suspended one leg over the side.

Peter protested. Slimy green algae clung to the pilings. He knew there was no way anyone could grip the scummy post without plunging headlong into the water. Franklin was a New Johnnie and

Peter did not really know him. He was three years younger than the fifteen year old and he was known for various risks he often took. Peter instinctively grabbed him by his shirt, "You're gonna get killed, Jackson." he warned. But the youth was aggressive when he wrenched himself away from Peter's grip and scrambled down toward the snarled fishing line. When halfway down he realized he had placed himself in jeopardy where slippery algae gave him no traction.

Dark, frightened eyes looked up at Peter who had now shimmed down the slimy piling while holding to the dry railing above. The older boy gripped Jackson by his shirt collar and jerked him upward where he dangled precariously over the water. Peter raged at the stupid boy. "Do that again you idiot and I'm gonna let you drown." With a monumental heave he pulled the unrestrained youth onto the pier.

Jackson lay sprawled on the wooden deck, gasping for breath where he was josled so violently.

"That was the dumbest thing I ever saw anyone do." Peter knelt next to the grinning daredevil.

The younger boy's smile glistened at his mentor, "I almost had it, Petee. Another foot and I woulda had it unhooked." his voice rose triumphantly.

A crowd gathered and watched in amusement at Jackson's expense. A bevy of voices brought catcalls at the ignorance of the youth. Peter stepped away from the crowd when a voice snarled, "You should've let the nigger drown." Pappas flew into a rage. He turned on the slandering scoundrel, "What's that you said?" he glared at the offender when suddenly the protagonist fisted a hard punch into Peter's ribs.

In an instant reaction Peter attacked his grinning adversary. The two fell to the pier, fists pummeling one another until calmer students pulled the opponents apart. A seething glare filled Pappas's eyes. In one last desperate insult his bleeding attacker snapped, "Jew lover! Nigger lover! Greek bastard!" It took strong hands to control the infuriated Peter who struggled to clash again with the offending troublemaker.

Peter stormed away from the lingering crowd. His ribs hurt and a cut on his elbow was stinging. A fragment of a torn pant leg fluttered from his right leg. Disheveled and hurting he quickened his pace toward the large barn; he wanted to be alone. From behind he heard someone running to catch up to him. Thinking his attacker was racing to finish the fight he turned on his heel, fists clenched, now ready to meet the challenge. When he turned his heart slowed rhythmically when the young Franklin slowed to walk and smiled sheepishly at his defender.

"Petee. thanks for sticking up for me." he puffed after chasing after the retreating protector. Peter rested his arm on the youth's shoulders and silently led him to the rear of the barn. His thoughts were rushing in every direction. He never thought any of the boys on the island could be that vicious. Jew lover! Nigger lover! The insults ravaged his brain for he had never heard such derogatory remarks since he left the tenement. He hated those terms when he was younger, but he was too frail, too small to do anything about it.

Finally he said, "It's okay, Franklin." He faced the younger boy and gripped him tightly around the shoulders. Looking intently into the questioning eyes of the youth, he continued, "Nobody! But nobody is ever gonna call you a nigger while I'm around." he said with finality.

Jackson winced from the smear. He met Peter's gaze evenly and then gave his defender a nervous snicker, "Ya'll's gonna have to stay here 'till I graduates, Petee." he mimicked, then giggled in pretense of not being offended, however, when he started to walk away he turned and said, "Petee, I've been called that since I can't remember." He waved to his friend and slipped around the corner of the barn.

Once the two youths parted Peter started out to see Miss Pederson. It was a lonely walk. Oddly, there were no crows anywhere. Yet, their muffled, all-powerful cries could still be heard from somewhere further than the farm house Peter thought it might be some kind of warning - perhaps one of the birds had been injured and the flock was on guard to protect the harmed member.

Finally, he arrived at his destination. He followed the well know path which led to the back porch. Off to the side Miss Pederson was studying a variety of plants all arranged in a neat row. An aromatic blend of budding fragrances from various shrubs lingered in a diverse bouquet of fragrances. "I'm glad you came, Petee." She said without turning for she recognized the boy's footsteps. She pointed her finger at the bench where Peter was to wait for her.

She was dressed in white slacks, accented by a pink chiffon blouse, highlighting her sunny smile. She looked beautiful with her shiny black hair was pulled back where a magenta ribbon tied off a pony tail. They spoke on vague, yet interesting items that could only stir the imagination of islanders. Pederson knew to bide her time. To wait until the boy was comfortable for he seemed troubled - anxious.

He seemd to drift away while trying to occupy his moments with the bowl of peanuts which by now was half empty. Soda followed in hurried sips. Miss Pederson eyed him curiously. Finally, if only to break the ice, she asked, "According to my calculations you're going to be sixteen next September, aren't you?" Her eyes fleetingly noted he looked very sloppy today, a trait he was unknown for. She knew better than to press him for answers.

He nodded an answer to her question while looking down at his scuffed shoes. Suddenly he volunteered, "I was in a fist fight today, ma-am." The muscles in his face twitched when he relived the brawl on the wharf.

She smiled thinly, "I see you have." She touched the tear in his pant leg, "I'll mend that for you."

Peter felt uneasy with her attention when he crossed one leg over the other as if to hide the tear. He frowned down at himself when he answered without looking at her, "It's okay, Miss Pederson. Someone in the sewing room will fix it."

Pederson dropped the matter of the pants and asked, "you mentioned a fight? Is that why you came out to see me." It was the only way she could think of to get the boy to relax and talk to her. When he mentioned he wanted to see her in the dining room that morning the fight had not happened yet. Her curiosity was building.

He refused her offer of more peanuts when he blurted, "Remember the game with Saint Paul's? I saw you there watching us." She nodded and waited. "Well, remember the catcher that tried to block the plate when I slid home and we crashed into each other?" In his eagerness to tell the story he turned so he faced her directly.

His eyes were fixed on hers and suddenly his gaze fell on her full lips, now pursed and pouted while she waited. The memory of Sheryl-Ann's kiss suddenly filled him with ecstasy. In that instant he wanted to touch his lips to his friend's, just like he did with Sheryl-Ann, only.... only, a foreboding swept the thought out of his mind. She trusted him.... he couldn't....he was ravaged by a guilt that he would ever think this way.

Turning away he hesitated awkwardly where his feelings clouded his thoughts. For an instant Pederson felt uncomfortable when his eyes lingered ever so hesitatingly upon her face. For the first time she felt a twinge of worry, but she quickly brushed the thought away. She then interrupted his reverie by asking, "And the catcher?" "What?" he asked in surprise.

"The catcher," she repeated, "You were telling me about the collision with the catcher." She smiled at how fragile the boy appeared. His discomfort was so obvious.

Peter lifted his eyes to her and shook his head in bewilderment, "Who?" he asked.

She smiled at his innocence and said, "You seem to be losing track of your story."

The boy pulled himself more erect on the bench. He felt his heart racing and then a slow blush filled his cheeks. She can see how embarrassed I am, he thought to himself. I'm blushing and she can see it. She knows what I'm thinking. His mind raced with his thoughts. Suddenly, he gulped deeply where he brought his senses back to reality and continued his account as he shook his head slowly, "He was on top of me and he said, "Are you the Jew boy?"

A simple, knowing smile crossed her lips. She nodded at the recognizable prejudice.

"And....And you know what I answered?" his voice was full of rage, "I told him to ask Jesus." his voice softened immediately when he continued, "And then I called him a hypocrite."

She nodded again and said, "That was a good answer, Peter."

When I told Feldman about it he told me a story about how his father got killed." An uneasy frown appeared on his forehead, "He said his father was killed because he was a Jew." A tortured look appeared on his youthful face. "And then....and then this afternoon," he continued, "Franklin tried to help me get my fishing line that snagged on a piling." he continued slowly, He came close to having an accident because he couldn't grip the piling that was filled with slippery algae. I grabbed him. I pulled with all my might and hauled him back onto the pier. He could've drowned."

And then all the other kids came around." He balled his fist and pounded it on his lap. "One of them said, "Why didn't you let the nigger drown." He bowed his head and turned away. Now feeling guilty he realized to whom he was using the word 'nigger'.

She placed her hand on his and asked, "Peter, did Feldman tell you what behavior is called?"

"Prejudice, ma-am." A scowl crossed his brow, "It's not right, Miss Pederson. Nobody should be called names like that. And that's why I beat him up." Fingering his torn pant leg he said, "That's how I got this."

She squeezed his hand then quickly released it. She wanted to comfort him and the only way she could this is to hold him in her arms - to try and ease the torture he was feeling. But, the thought would be impossible. It would only make worse a situation she did not want to find herself in. "Peter," she continued, "there are people in this world who can be very vicious. They don't care who they hurt by calling them names, because, some people are a little different. After awhile it begins to eat their insides out." She gave him a controlled smile when she continued, "Some people are yellow, others are red and still others are colored." She looked at him tenderly and said with finality, "Just like me."

She had turned and faced the boy directly, now wondering if her words were sinking in. "Some day, Peter, we'll be able to live our lives in some kind of harmony. A harmony...." She searched for an example and her voice modulated when she cultivated an instance. "A harmony like the music you play in the school band. Not all the instruments are alike. They all play different sounds. But, when they blend together they play harmonious music. They're in harmony. And....And some day all people will live like that." She paused for a moment, thinking and wishing it could all come true one day.

Peter's soft blue eyes circled her face only to linger with his deep thoughts. He then asked, "Miss Pederson? Did anyone ever call you names like that? He held his breath while waiting for an answer. Maybe he went too far with his question. He was not sure and he was now uncomfortable with what he had asked.

She gave him a quick, uneasy smile when she met his inquisitive gaze evenly and answered, "Yes, Peter. Even I've been insulted that way." Peter exhaled slowly when he turned away from the bench and slowly strode to a rose bush. He turned and looked at her sadly, "Miss Pederson," he hesitated when he kicked a stone away, now watching it skitter away noisily in a corner. His eyes followed the skittering rock and then with his eyes turned at the earth his voice soften when he asked, "Miss Pederson, can I kiss you?" Once again he sucked in his breath for he was sure he had put their friendship in trouble. Exhaling slowly he watched her leave the bench and walk over to him. A shiver of excitement raced through him.

When she approached she smiled at the emotional youth and reluctantly placed her arm around his shoulders. Peter felt a tremor race through him when she finally said, "Come walk with me, Petee. I think it's time we should talk." She smiled at the emotional youth, now looking at him thoughtfully. As she guided him along the path toward the dirt road her mind raced at the thought of her vulnerability.

She felt uncomfortable for now she realized Peter was not that naive young boy she met years earlier. He was growing into a young man who must be feeling all the desires of youthful fantasy. She knew she was vulnerable living alone in this large farm house, but this was not a time to feel threatened or defenseless. After a short walk she said, 'I know how you meant that desire to kiss me, Peter.

And do you know what you just did for me?" She eyed him directly. A trace of a tear glistened behind long eyelashes. "Petee, you may not realize it, but you gave me the nicest compliment a young man can give a woman." She smiled condescendingly while guiding him skillfully along the path leading away from the house.

Peter smiled at the compliment she too gave him while keeping pace with her disciplined lead. He knew there would never be a time that she would ever allow him to kiss her, after all, she was an adult who was also governed by rules. This much he knew. When they arrived at the dirt road which led back to the main campus she turned and said, "As for the kiss. Can that wait until your graduation?" Peter's mood brightened when he answered, "It's gonna be a long wait, Miss Pederson."

He trotted away with a wave at the scientist who always made him feel good about himself whenever he left her. He paced himself through the orchard where the fruited trees filled the air with blended aromas. Bursting delicate white flowers often reminded him of millions of white moths ready to ambush him. An now, to his right, fleshy dark cherries clung to tees that were ready for harvesting. He was tempted to taste a few, but the thought of a demerit was not worth the chance.

The weighty smell of corn silage mixed with the aroma of depleting hay in the lofts signaled a warning he had entered the region where milking cows rested after their day in the pastures. He noticed the cow barn door had been left ajar, obviously the fault of a careless farm boy. From behind the door an appalling, distressed roar blared loudly from an animal in great pain. Peter gulped nervously when he swung the door open and to his amazement he saw a pair of man's legs jutting from behind the reclined bawling cow.

He swallowed deeply, then called out loudly so he could be heard above the pain racked animal. "Mister Armbrewster?" For now he recognized the head farmer struggling with the writing animal. The adults arms looked as though they were shoved through the cow's birth channel and all the way into the belly of the distraught creature. A sweaty face looked in surprise when he saw Peter. "Pappas," he snapped, "Roll up your sleeves and get down here. I need your help." His voice rose above the piercing cries of the panicky cow.

Peter looked aghast where Armbrewster expected him to prostrate himself behind the repugnant and odor-filled yet offensive chore of helping a cow give up a difficult birth. The frightened boy dropped to his knees while keeping a wary eye on the thrashing legs of the pitiful animal. "Reach in here, Pappas." Arbrewster made way for the lad whose face had now turned ashen. Trembling hands followed those of the Instructor and in seconds he too found his shoulder pressed against the cow, his hand groping for some unknown source.

"She's in trouble, Peter." the head farmer gasped for air between grunts of his own from the difficult task. "Reach far into the vulva." The orders were quick and demanding. "Go as far as you can into the womb until you can feel the calf. She's got a calf in breach and we've got to help her." The boy dared not disobey despite strange questions as to what is breach? What is a vulva? A womb? And what the hell am I doing here?" Everything was foreign to him even if he did work the barn when he was a lot younger. Too bad Bix wasn't there to help him, he thought.

"Can you feel the calf?" Armbrewster's voice sounded as if it came from somewhere under the writing creature..

"I can feel something slimy, sir." Peter tried holding his breath, but it was hopeless as the smells seemed to intensify.

"You've got the birth-sack," Armbrewster counseled, "Press your fingers into it. Do you feel the calf?

"Yes! Yes!" he shouted elatedly when his fingers touched the birthing animal, "I can feel the calf, sir. It's wriggling!" A broad smile was fixed on his face. He had conquered something, yet he was still overwhelmed with the activity. Suddenly, he grimaced in pain when he yelled that the cow had twisted and her weight lay heavily on his shoulder. He tried to pull from under her, only, to find it hopeless. "Push, Peter. Push the calf toward me." The boy pressed with all his strength, "Is anything happening, sir?"

"Yes we're turning it. Keep pushing, lad." In one second the boy looked over at Armbrewster who was sweating profusely, "Sir! It's gone! I can't feel the calf." Panic filled his voice, 'Maybe it's in the cow's throat!"

"It's okay, Petee. We've turned it." Armbrewster chuckled when he pulled his arm away and sat squatting on his haunches. "Now watch out. It's going to be born."

The warning came too late. Peter's shoulder was still trapped with the weight of the mother. Suddenly, a slimy mass dropped onto his pants - a gooey glob lay fully against Peter's thighs. The boy's eyes dropped into a stirring gaze where agitated movements filled the birth sack. He stared dumbfounded at Mister Armbrewster who was now standing off to one side waiting for the cow who would pursue and ancient ritual of caring for her baby.

A desperate cry from the calf brought up a warm smile for the still pinioned Peter. The heifer struggled to her feet which finally released the pinned arm. The teen squirmed away and sat on the cement walkway for warm attentive eyes brought a simple smile of accomplishment to the youth who had been thrust into a miracle of birth.

"Is it a girl or a boy, Mister Armbrewster?" he asked inquisitively.

The adult smiled down at the incredulous youth, 'I think it's a calf, Petee." he winked and chuckled at his own joke.

The boy's eyes flicked from the struggling calf, who was now being licked clean by the mother, and back to the farmer, "That's a girl cow, isn't it. sir?" For Peter it was a serious question and he failed to see Armbrewster's humor. Rather than keep the young man in suspense any longer it was agreed by both participants it was indeed a girl cow.

The emergency was over. Peter looked down at his stained shirt and hastily pulled it off. He showed his disdain of the sour smells by tossing his shirt to one side, wishing he had known earlier how distasteful helping a cow with a breached birth could be. The two washed at a farm animal's drinking trough. Peter remembered that this was the same trough Bix and Headmaster Williamson used after they helped the cow and the bull that so frightened the New Johnnie.

He grinned broadly when he was complimented for helping with the emergency. Now he had something exciting to tell his friend Feldman. But questions were now nagging him when finally he asked, "Sir, what's a vulva?" The adult did not answer right away. The boy continued, "What's a breach? And....And what's a womb?" he waited for an answer expectantly.

Armbrewster's brow wrinkled into a frown. He wondered if it was proper for him to answer these questions since they were the type questions that should be answered in a classroom. And then, a thought crossed his mind, "Son, you're about to go into what grade in school?" The inquisitive youth explained he was about to enter into his sophomore year. He wondered what that had to do with his questions.

A creeping contented smile appeared on the adult. "Isn't it the sophomore year when you begin science classes?" he asked hopefully. "Oh, yea," the boy answered, only to suddenly scowl when he remembered the older boys telling him they would be studying bugs. "You know. Mister Armbrewster Sir, I ain't gonna be that interested in studying bugs."

Armbrewster looked up at the sky while rocking back and forth on his heels. His hands were in his pockets where his fingers toyed with loose change. "Well, son, it's not going to be all about bugs. Later in the year you're going to be studying animals and humans, aren't you?" Peter nodded his agreement. Smiling slyly Armbrewster clapped the youth on his shoulder and ended the conversation by saying, "Well, my boy, you can ask your teacher about these things you want to know. Spirited by his cleverness at avoiding an uncomfortable discussion the adult walked away.

It was Monday afternoon when Peter and Isaiah sat on a bench at the baseball diamond. They watched and identified various camouflaged ships leaving the port of Boston, a hobby every boy on the island mastered by naming the type cargo held in the holds of the vessel. "Gees, Ike, looka there. That's a tanker coming out and boy is she loaded." Feldman squinted at the lumbering craft and pointed out the huge blue and white stripes designed to disguise it from lurking enemy submarines.

They sat quietly while the low slung tanker made its way through the harbor. Isaiah nervously fidgeted with a short stick, slapping it on his lap then twisted it in his hands. Peter quickly noticed his friend's attitude when he asked, "What'ya doing, Ike, killing mosquitoes with that stick?" Feldman smiled, but did not answer. Finally he lay the distractiion aside then slowly wiped his glasses with a handkerchief.

Peter's concern forced a frown upon his brow. He had seen his friend's various moods and somehow the two of them worked out a problem. But, this time, he sensed something more dramatic in the way Ike was behaving. "Somethings bugging you today, huh Ike. Ya wanna talk about it?" His friend shoved his legs under the bench letting his shoes score various lines in the dirt.

"It's my mother, Petee." he finally blurted, "She did something stupid like getting married again. And now....And now I was told I have to leave the school because I've got two parents and that goes against the, you know, the rules." He stood up abruptly and shoved his hands into his pants pockets then kicked a stone so it tumbled violently against the baseball backstop. Turning to face his friend he said, "I've got to be off the island tomorrow." His eyes glistened when he turned his back and looked out at the harbor.

Peter stared dumbfounded. Troubled shifting eyes were locked on Isaiah. His mouth frowned into a gimace when he stood next to his distraught friend. For the moment he was stunned where words were escaping him. He felt the pain in this upcoming rupture of their friendship and the only thing he could do at the moment was place his hand on Feldman's shoulder

His voice was now plaintive when he said, "I know the rules are strict about a student coming here who couldn't afford the tuition and having lost one of his parents with the damned death and this damned divorce and the damn separation shit."

Without turning Feldman said, "I've got a father now. I've got a step-father, he immediately corrected. My mother is married. I don't come under the rules of death, divorce or separation." He turned and looked at Peter with troubled eyes. 'Petee, my days on the island are finished, that's all." He returned to the bench and sat down wearily.

"It's not fair!" Peter's shouted his disapproval while punching his fist into the air. "Damn, Ike, it just ain't fair!" He clamped his hands between his knees and stared doggedly at the ground.

Isaiah rubbed Peter's back and said, "We're still friends for life, aren't we Petee? We did kiss on it, didn't we? And it doesn't mean we can't still be friends with me over there and you here.

"Yea, I guess so." Peter answered wearily. "I guess we can write to each other, huh, Ike." He suddenly warmed to the subject, "And you can come on visitor's day to see me. And....And when I come home I'll call you and we can go to movies and stuff like that." Suddenly he frowned at himself and volunteered, "Jeez Ike, we ain't got a phone. My Dad can't afford one. But....but I'll use a public phone instead." He smiled at his own ability to solve the problem.

Isaiah kicked a cinder from the oval track, the rough hewn stone skittered away, clattering like an escaping mouse. "Will you come to the dock and see me off tomorrow, Petee?" he asked. His friend choked on his attempt to speak and then simply nodded his head.

It was the next day. The nine o'clock boat had already reached the dock at Boston's City Point, Isaiah was gone. Peter sat alone on the bench surrounding the old elm tree. He felt empty, like the day Ralph Benson was buried and also when his friend Bix left to join the submarines, and now Isaiah joins the list. Peter chuckled to himself when he suddenly remembered inadvertently giving Feldman his nickname. Oh, how quickly that name stuck. And then he remembered how they made such fools of themselves at the class presentation - it was the two of them sticking their necks out - always together. And then the kiss that sealed their loyalty to each other.

Their farewell at the dock that morning was awkward. Peter felt so hollow and he could see his friend's lips tighten, a brooding gaze silently blended with Petee's own numbed stare. He wanted to hug Isaiah, but no one would understand and then the whole school would know about it and he would be teased. He was sure Ike understood. Feldman always said shaking hands was a "klutsy" way to say goodbye. It brought back the memory when Isaiah first used "klutsy". A Hebrew insult meaning stupid or dull. He forgot why.

They shook hands. Neither spoke for a moment and then they silently smiled back at each other when suddenly each spoke simultaneously, "Klutsy, ain't it?" An impish giggle poured from both when Peter's hand released from Isaiah's and the two friends parted. From the stern of the boat Ike looked up at the forlorn figure staring down from the dock. Each flashed a flattered smile to one another when Peter turned and walked away slowly.

Reliving that moment of parting Peter failed to notice a young boy sitting next to him. "Hi Petee." a cheerful, high-spirited voice interrupted his reverie. Annoyed with the intrusion Pappas snapped, "Jackson, what are you doing here? Why aren't you in class?" The youngster dangled his feet off the bench and swirled them in the air, "I've got a measle." he announced proudly while pumping his legs back and forth. "See!" he pointed to a small, red, infectious and yet, communicable dot on his cheek.

Peter jumped to his feet, taking a few steps back, "You've got measles and you're sitting next to me?" he glared stonily at the youthful offender.

"Yup!" Jackson answered proudly, "See this?" once again he pointed to the offensive red spot on his cheek, "That's a measle and teacher's sending me to the "firmary. Ahm a sick boy," he grinned like a Cheshire cat, "this here's measle is all mine. They's gonna keep me out of class." He pumped his arms up and down as if he had just scored a touchdown..

"Yours! Yours!" Peter's voice rose excitedly. A Stony look met the open, youthful face of the grinning boy. "You're a klutz! You hear me? You're a klutz!" he repeated while backing away.

The youngster suddenly became somber when he saw panic in Peter, "I won't give 'em to ya...." he hesitated and then grinned, "so long's ya come to the firmery and see me?" He took a step toward Petee who by now had distanced himself from the infected student. "Petee?" he asked innocently, "What's a klutz?"

"Never mind!" Peter snapped, "Now get your ass to the infirmary."

The youngster turned away only to turn back like a pesky mosquito and faced the agitated teenager, "When ya comes visits me, Petee, will you tell me what a klutz is?"

The infected boy somberly walked away with his hands clasped behind him. Peter stared after him, wondering if the brief contact would give him measles again. He remembered his twin sister and himself getting chicken pox and maybe catching measles. But can you catch the dreaded chicken pox and measles after you've had chicken pox? The question hung grimly in his mind. Suddenly, from a distance he heard, "Petee, are you mad at me?" The teenager threw his up hands in disbelief. He bowed his head as if in prayer and then looked at the disheveled boy waiting for an answer. Smiling to himself he finally said, "No Jackson. I'm not mad at you. Now get your butt to the infirmary and I'll be up to see you when the nurse lets me." A bright smile sparkled back, "I'll be waitin', Petee. You'll know where to find me, huh?" A final wave and he walked away.

CHAPTER TWELVE

A DISASTER

Peter entered the shed which held all the garden tools. It was time he began his required four hour work time-table. With classes in the afternoon and band practice scheduled for the evening it did not leave him much time and so planning his activities was very important. His detail called for weeding the flower gardens in front of each dormitory which meant he would be aching from all the stooping and kneeling. With a cultivator in one hand and a trowel in the other he sprinted across the quadrangle to the Thomas House dormitory.

It was in Thomas House where the older boy were quartered. Those nearing graduation were housed to his right in Bowditch House. Here the dining hall and kitchens occupied the entire first floor. The rest of the Bowditch second floor held the infirmary along with the senior's rooms. To his left and making up the quadrangle was Baxter House and Albee House. Albee House quartered the younger boys with the others progressively housed by age.

Peter knelt into the bed and yanked out weeds, then churned the soil with the cultivator. It was the only job he disliked when working the landscape department and yet, when it was finished a proper harmony of greens and budding flowers complimented the buildings. The boy wondered if anyone really noticed. Shiny ivy vines traced up bare walls toward the windows where their tentacles clung to crevasses between the red bricks, now blending into green velvet leaves. Peter promised himself that after he graduated he would visit the island if only to see the ivy scene which would make the school quadrangle look like a sleepy village.

He was busy finishing the work in front of Albee House when he was startled by a strange man's voice that said, "You've a gifted hand, laddie." In that instant the boy's eyes widen in alarm. He shot a curious look at a strange, disheveled old man who leaned a trembling hand on a warped cane for support. Stay silver hair dangled loosely from under a Greek fisherman's hat that accented half glasses clutched to the tip of his nose. The old man's jaw quivered when he removed a curved smokeless pipe couched in the corner of his mouth. He then smiled toothlessly at the surprised youth.

Peter bit his lower lip curiously for he wondered who on earth this could be. The boy stood and found his own height matched that of the old man. 'Th....the....thank you, sir. he responded to the compliment given him a few moments ago. His eyes drifted to the clumsy looking walking stick whose handle was squeezed tightly by gnarled fingers, without which the shabby, unshaven man would certainly tumble to the ground.

"It's called a shillelagh." He volunteered while twirling the the stick slowly.

Peter gave him a faultering smile, "Can I hold your cane, sir?" he asked innocently.

The old man leaned forward with a pale blank face and abruptly said, "Oh no! Young feller. Ya must nevah touch another man's shillelagh." He blinked nervously and pursed trembling lips when he leaned closer still and said, "Touching another man's shillelagh can bring bad luck, don't' cha-know?" He stared at the boy with frozen, unblinking eyes which instantly softened. He then stared off as if recalling an event in his life in the years past.

"Bad luck, sir?" Peter interrupted the old man's reverie.

Jolted by the question the old man raised a frustrated brow and smiled toothlessly at the inquisitive boy. "Ayuh, real bad luck." He whispered now, forcing Peter to squint while trying to hear. "One time thar was this heya woman who kicked a boarder outa house and flung his confounded shillelagh after him." He winked at the curious youth and continued, "She should'na done that son, cause bad luck was sartin to follow the old hag. The old man took a quick look over his shoulder as if to satisfy himself no one else could hear. He stepped closer and continued, "Ya see laddie her son became a thief and stole an egg. He brought the egg to his mother and she didn't say nary a word to him 'bout where he got it. He then stole the chicken and , his mother didn't say nary a word."

Peter felt uncomfortable when the old man took a step closer. A foul tobacco smell passed his nose. But the old man continued, now wrapped up with the story, "Thet boy stole all kinds of things. Bigger, more expensive things, ya hear me boy?" He nodded tight-lipped at the youth. "And then one day he got hisself ketched. Jest like thet chicken he stole."

He chuckled where he was swept up telling the tale, now arching his right eyebrow forcing the eyeball into a grape size glare. "They was gunna hang the theivin bum." He was now grinning demonically where Peter stared back at the unblinking eye. "The hanging man says to him, "Ya got anything to say fore we spring the trap?'"

I could barely hear the dang no good bum when he asks, "I wanna speak to me mudder."

The old man's jaw quivered into a snappish, broiling spasm of laughter - cackling loudly at the bewildered Peter who stood riveted in place. "He wants to speak to his mudder, he asks. This bum, this no good teef wants to speak to his mudder. Ha!" he bellowed when he jammed his shellelagh into the earth and giving it a twist into the soil.

Peter shifted his gaze from the story teller for the glaring eyeball made him uncomfortable. He thought for sure it would drop out of its socket. And then it quickly slipped behind squinting eyes which stayed focused on the boy. "When his mudder comes he asks her to come close so he could whisper in her ear. In a flash, my boy, the teef chawed down her ear with his teeth. The old hag lets out a almighty scream even God and all his Angels in Heaven could hear.

Peter stared dumbfounded at the story teller who continued, "Ha!" he bellowed again, "He would-na let go thet ear 'till the strong hangman yanked her away. "Thets cuz ya didn't whomp me fer stealing thet egg." Peter gave the old man a quick, easy smile at reaching the ending of the preposterous narrative when suddenly Coach Johnson arrived. "I see you've met Mister Angus Derry from South Boston, Petee." The old man draped a sweaty arm around Peter's shoulder and said, "The lad listens to my stories. That makes him a fine young-un."

Peter looked at the Coach who explained how the old man was telling him about his shillelagh when the man cackled and interrupted, "Aye and ye never touch another man's shellelah now, do you son?" He turned abruptly and as he shuffled away he waved the crooked cane in the air now mumbling incoherently. His curious cackle could still be heard when he rounded a dormitory and plodded along to the waiting Pilgrim at the dock.

The Coach explained to the astonished Peter how the old man often came to the island with his fantastic stories. He went on to say how he suddenly disappeared and had not been seen these past few years. He assumed the storyteller may have died, but now with this surprise visit it was nice to find him very much alive. Despite the old man's peculiarities Angus Derry's history involved seamanship on old freighters that plied the seas. Now his memories of adventures were often spiced and seasoned to everyone's amusement.

It was a week later when Peter climbed the stairs to the Bowditch House infirmary. With the other boys either attending classes or working there was a strange stillness in the hall. A curious smell of antiseptics brought reality that somewhere on this floor illnesses were cured and boys were eventually freed from the confinement. Peter checked with the nurse for permission to enter the infirmary and here she nodded imperceptibly in agreement. Peter detested being mollified in this manner only to quickly swallow his pride and enter the infirmary.

The door opened silently to Peter's touch for now he found Jackson sound asleep, the only patient in the large room. Blemishes from healing pockmarks were still visible on his silky black skin. The visitor noiselessly closed the door, then sat ever so carefully on the edge of the bed where an creak from the bed instantly rooted the teenager in place. He cast a quick look at the youngster who lay sleeping, still undisturbed, but Petee was not too sure that someone might be deceiving him. He crossed his arms and smiled down at his friend.

The sleeping boy suddenly shifted in bed where he kicked his visitor which awakened him instantly. Sleepy eyes looked in bewilderment and suddenly his jaw dropped open in surprise. A gleaming smile filled his face as he raised himself on one elbow. "PETEE!" he shouted with joy. "YOU CAME!" His voiced echoed in the vast room. Peter's smile equaled the boy's who reached out to grasp his visitor. But, Peter pulled back and said, "I'm not sure I can touch you." The youngster chuckled, "You can touch me, Petee. Looka," he shouted when holding up his arm, "There ain't no measel on me, ycept a few thing-stuffs on my face."

"Thing-stuffs." Peter mocked.

"Yea, looka the thing-stuffs on my face. The nurse says when they goes away I can leave." His eyes brightened at the thought he would gain his freedom once again.

"You've been lonely, huh, Jackson." Peter teased.

"Yea," he answered quickly, "And you know what was worser?" His brow turned into a deep scowel, "Teacher gave me lessons now that I'm better. Looka," he pointed to three books next to his bed, "Yuk! Geography," he grunted, "and math and, and, English."

Peter kicked off his shoes where they landed with a loud thump on the floor. Stretching his arms so his hands cradled his head he recalled the visit he had earlier by the old man from South Boston. Jackson was enthralled when he explained the shillelagh and the mystery it involved. Then he told him about the stolen egg and what happened to the thief. "I gotta meet this guy." Jackson interrupted.

"Ya know Petee, my Daddy was a lot like that. I member some stories he used to tell me." He drifted off in thought for a moment and continued, "My Daddy got himself killed in the army. They told me he got killed in a invasion in some place called Italy." Teary eyes met Peter's fixed stare. "Why did they go kill him for?" He burst into sobs when Peter wrapped his arms around the weeping boy. Their cheeks touched when Jackson blurted in a broken sentence, "Now.... ya gonna get my measel, Petee," he sniffed noisily,...."cuz your cheek touched mine." He laughed at his own silliness while wiping the salty tears away with his hands. The memory of his father was now tucked into some special niche of his mind.

"Did you lose your Dad like me, Petee?" Sad eyes looked for an answer.

Peter felt uncomfortable for his father was very much alive, however, there was the memory of Ralph which lingered in his mind. He remembered the first time he met the boy who would be his closest friend. They were New Johnies when Peter asked Mister Cliford some stupid questions about fire escapes in the main building where they would be sleeping that night. He felt so dumb and embarrassed in front of all the new kids.

The group walked to the dining room and next too him a boy with a limp struggled to keep pace. The first thing out of that boy's mouth was a wisecrack laced with a swear and aimed at Peter. Something like 'You stepped in a pile of shit kid.' Peter could not remember the exact smear, but he took an instant dislike to that boy for once again he was embarrassed in front of all the other new kids.. Jackson interrupted his thoughts when he repeated his question about Peter's Dad.

"Naa, I didn't lose my Dad like you did." he answered, "But, I did lose my best friend." He smiled to himself at the absurdity of first hating someone and now, upon reflection, how they became the best of friends. He grinned at the inquisitive young boy and said, "He's even buried in the graveyard at the south end of the island." "Is it the same thing, Petee? Did you love him. too?

The question caught Peter completely off guard. He flashed back to the times he and Ralph spent together. A cascade of memories flooded his thoughts. There were so many times that Ralph put Peter in situations where he would surely be put in detention if they got caught. Why they never got caught still puzzled him. He was amazed that despite his friend's leg infirmity they got in situations where they could have gotten hurt or even killed for that matter. The thought of being killed clung grimly. His eyes suddenly glazed over, tears were held back when he turned his head away from Jackson who stared at him wide-eyed for an answer to his simple question.

The fifteen year old felt a lump in his throat. He gasped for a quick breath of air and he then left the younger boy's bed and looked out the window as far down as the football field in the distance and then further to the busy harbor. He rubbed away tears that slipped down his cheeks. It was a moment the senior boy needed to refocus his thoughts, to stifle his need to cry. From behind a worried voice broke the silence, "Petee? Are you okay?"

Peter shook his head in an affirmative assent. And then an unrestrained impulse gripped him when he realized he did indeed love his friend. He was uncomfortable at the thought for he never realized that other than family, two young boys could truly love each other. Now controlling his emotions he returned to Jackson's bed and smiled respectfully at the questioning young boy when he answered softly, "Yea, Jackson, I did love him." He finally found the right expression to describe his hidden feelings. Feelings that were subtly suppressed, subtly confused for such a long time. "I really, really did love him."

The young boy squirmed onto his knees, his excitement radiated from a broad smile. Questions poured like an incoming tide flooding a beach, "Where is he? What's his name? Is he really buried in the island cemetery? Was he a student? The raging questions were overwhelming. "And, and, how did he die, Petee? Peter's laughter filled the room. He tickled the inquiring youth where giddy shrieks pierced the infirmary. "Ya gotta take me there? he begged. "Did he get killed in Italy too?"

Peter felt uncomfortable by the prodding boy expecting some thoughtless adventure over the death of his friend Ralph. His only thought was to change the subject when he asked, "You know Jackson I've always called you Jackson. What's your first name. Do you have one? he asked jokily. A dimpled smile appeared on the adolescents face when he asked solemnly, "Ya promise not to laugh, Petee?"

Peter draped his arm over the boy's small shoulder and said, "I promise. Honest I will."

The youngster hesitated a moment and then answered, "It's Leopold." The youth's voice was barely above a whisper. He pulled away from Peter's arm and squatted on the bed Indian style, crossed legs with his arms folded. A grim expression filled his face as though he were about to challenge any mockery.

Peter instinctively snickered, "Leopold!" he repeated when he turned his face away so the boy would not see his lips clamped to suppress a laugh.

Jackson glared at his mentor, "You promised you wouldn't laugh, Petee." A stern, challenging look appeared on his face.

The older boy cupped his hand over his mouth and blurted, "I'm not laughing, Jackson, honest," and then he looked quizzically, "but Leopold?" he repeated questioningly.

"I shouldn'a told you, huh, Petee." he snapped when he yanked his covers and pulled them over his knees. A sullen pout was fixed severely on his face.

Peter faced the boy with a controlled voice and said, "Hey, Jackson, does it really look like I'm laughing?" He bit his lower lip to restrain another chuckle, "But, Leopold!" he blurted as he burst out laughing. He grabbed the angry youth, now wrestling with the defensive boy who screeched when the youth wrapped his arms around Peter's neck and threatened, "I'm gonna give you a measel, Petee. And then you'll be stuck in this firmery too."

They wrestled on the bed until Peter pinned the arms of the struggling youngster. "And I bet you can't guess my middle name, Le-o-pold!" he dragged out the name purposely when he challenged the giggling boy about his own middle name. He relaxed his grip on Jackson and said in a false stern voice, "And you better not laugh or ya gonna stay in this firmery with a broken head." he mocked his friend's language.

"Okay! Okay!, he begged, "I promise not to laugh." A sly I'm-gonna-get-you look crossed his face, "Tell me, Petee, what's you middle name?" he asked.

Peter eyed him suspiciously and then he continued, "It's - It's," he hesitated and then said, "It's Haralambos."

"WHAT!" The youth's voice rose hysterically. "You're name's WHAT!" He shrieked with laughter, "Harala WHAT! Harala WHO!" Peter grabbed the pillow and playfully smothered the youngster's face, "You promised you wouldn't laugh!" His voice rose in a faked scorn. Peter grinned broadly behind the pretense of being angry. "Harala WHAT!" Jackson continued his harrasment until his challenger pinioned the boy once again, "Listen to me you fibber," he snarled, "My name's Haralambos and it means Harold in Greek. Now what does L-L-L-Leo-pold bumbeopold, teelegged tilegged bowlegged L-L-L-Leo-pold mean?"

"I ain't bowlegged." he retorted when Peter released his hold on the boy. "My Mom's a history teacher and she named me after some bigwig king from Belgium or Germany or some place like that." Suddenly, the door to the infirmary opened where a starched white uniformed nurse pointed a finger at Peter and brusquely ordered, "You! Take a hike. You're out of here." As gruff as it sounded it meant no harm. Peter took the cue and left. "See ya Leopold." he tossed the goodbye as a simple off-the-cuff remark.

The days passed rapidly for Peter. Graduation had sent another group of boys home to begin new lives. He was an up-coming high school junior this year. Now, summer offered freedom from classes. He was soon at the beach, sitting on a beached driftwood log next to the wharf where he watched the yachts whose propellers churned waters that frothed into a bubbly, hissing spray where the sun's rays filtered a shower of rainbow of colors. Summer thrill seekers filled the bay on that June day in 1945.

Driftwood, like the piece he sat on, had been brought to shore by violent winter storms - aggressive nor'easter blizzards thundered onto to the seashore. Ruthless white capped waves reminded one of white-maned lions surging toward helpless prey. And now it was summer where the rich, salty air overwhelmed delicate senses enveloped in a profusion of invasive moist odors that were now mixed into a blend of woody smells from the drying driftwood.

Thinking into the past, Peter recalled his first day when he was left alone at City Point to wait for the boat which would take him to his new island home. He was fearful, anxious and nervous and yet anything would have been better than the hated tenement which he called home. He wondered if could ever do it again. His reverie was suddenly interrupted when he was grasped from behind. Black hands gripped his shoulders when a voice said, "How's Harala, today." A infectious giggle met Peter's hunched shoulders. "It can only be my friend Leopold from the firmery." Peter said without turning, "The nasty kid who wanted to give me his measel."

"I saw you from the wharf," the youngster explained when he sat next to the older boy.

Peter rubbed Jackson's hair when the lad pulled away and said, "You mussing my hair." Peter laughed, then answered, "But your hair's all curly. How can I mess up your hair?" The youngster patted the top of his head, "That's why I don't hafta comb it." he wisecracked. "You like to tease me, huh, Petee? Saucer eyes met Peter's smile. But the question was ignored when the now sixteen year old pointed toward the south end of the island, "See that white house away down there beyond the root cellar?" Jackson squinted into the distance, "Well, the lady that lives there is a special friend of mine."

"You mean Miss Pederson?" he asked.

"Yea. And on the other side of the house is the cemetery where my friend Ralph Benson is buried."

Jackson reached into the sand and swirled his fingers through the loose granules. He rested his chin on top of his knees and asked, "Will you show me his grave, Petee?"

Either Peter did not hear the question or he simply ignored it for his mind had drifted. He was bringing back the memory of Ralph Benson. A frown suddenly appeared on his forehead for how could he put aside that tragic day in the barn without feeling the grief of that day. Two young friends causing innocent mischief catapulted them into a turmoil beyond belief.

"Will you show me his grave?" Jackson interrupted the sadness of his friend.

Peter took a few steps away, then turned and said, "Come-on Leopold, Let's go to the cemetery and I'll introduce you to Ralph."

The boy stuttered and said, "What do you mean, Petee. Ain't he. I mean he's dead, ain't he? He rushed to keep pace with the quick stepping youth. "Hey Petee." he stopped trying to keep up. Peter turned, now knowing what was troubling Jackson. He smiled mischievously and asked, "What?"

"You can't introduce me to a dead guy. Even I know that." "I talk to him all the time." Peter continued walking as the confused youngster followed. But Jackson, not to be fooled shouted "Yea, right!

They approached the orchard where they frightened a flock of crows. The huge black birds filled the air in a display of indignation, cawing their displeasure raucously that anyone would dare disturb their rest. The enormous birds followed their leader in a haphazard formation while chattering unhappily for now the resonance became more distant. Somewhere at the south end of the island they would once again settle amongst the trees and await some other eruption. Peter remembered the days when he first came to the school and for the first time heard crows - they startled him at the time since he never saw any bird that size flying or roosting anywhere near the tenement where he lived. For that matter no trees grew where in the summer's steaming hot cement sidewalks and tarred roads controlled peoples lives. The boy hated where he lived.

His thoughts brought a simple smile to his face when he recalled the day when he and his friend Ralph stood at this very spot in the orchard. His companion rebuked the young Peter's innocence for everything seemed to frighten the lad. He turned to Jackson who was standing by his side and pointed at the barn and was about to tell him of his experience with the wheelbarrow when suddenly his face paled. His jaw dropped open in horror, "Hey, look there ! Jackson, do you see it? It's smoke!" he shouted, "It's coming from the barn!"

"What'll we do, Petee?" the youngster's voice rose hysterically.

The orders came swiftly from the older boy when he shouted, "Run to the main building and pull the rope on the fire bell. Keep ringing it until the whole school knows the barn's on fire!" Gray, pungent smoke was now pouring out the cow barn as Peter raced in that direction. He knew most of the cows were grazing out to pasture, but the babies - the baby cows were kept indoors. A flash of fire blew out a window just when Peter arrived, but the intense heat prevented him getting any closer. Gritting his teeth in frustration he turned away where he pinched his tear filled eyes at the loss of the innocent infants.

In the distance the sounds of the huge fire bell tolled urgently. At least help would be on its way, but with the barn full of hay what could possibly save the structure. Suddenly, he remembered the horses on the second floor. He saw that the fire had not reached that section. But now panic from the powerful animals brought whinnies of fear for they were secured by leather halters in their stalls. In their terror four of the magnificent brutes could surely crush anyone trying to help them.

But Peter threw caution to the wind when he gripped a sharp sickle and entered an empty stall next to the nearest bolting horse. The smoke was now overwhelming as the boy leaned over the wall of the empty stall, his extended his arm with the sickle sliced at the deadly halter. Instantly, the horse disappeared out the huge barn doors. As speedily as he could the sixteen year old cut the remaining three horse's leather tethers so they too escaped.

Smothering his nose and mouth with his hands the boy charged toward the massive barn doors. In that instant he suddenly felt the fear he had when he was a child in the fire that almost killed his family. But now, there was no time to think about that for he was blinded by the smoke inside the cavernous barn. He stumbled, falling to his knees where he discovered enough air at the floor to help him breath as he crawled safely out the door. Firm hands gripped the gasping Peter and was hauled away from the rapidly dissolving structure.

Staring up through smarting eyes he faintly saw the hulking figure of Headmaster Williamson who was surrounded by so many other people. Ever so slowly the exhausted youth was breathing normally when he heard the stern voice of his superior say, "That was very foolish of you young man." The severe face looking down upon him slowly smiled when he continued, "It was also very brave of you to free those horses. We're all very proud of you, Peter."

It was some days later where down at the remnants of the fire ravaged barn heavy bulldozers scoured away the cindered debris. During the inferno a fleet of fire boats which were guarding Boston's harbor were dispatched to Thompson's Island then flooded the inferno with torrents of salt water dredged from the sea. Nothing remained of the once princely domain which housed so much livestock that had been cared for by eager teenagers who throughout the years educated them in the principals of animal husbandry with the guidance of adults. Now, this method of leadership would be but a memory to all those young adults who had labored so hard to gain knowledge in pursuit of an education.

A lonely boy sat on a high rock ledge by the barn - a ledge which originally formed an enclosed walkway for cows, goats and horses leading out to the pastures. There was an empty feeling inside Peter where his memories reflected back to the days when he was first assigned to work the farm. An innocent, inquisitive thirteen year old city boy plunged into unheard of daily chores that would be thrust upon him.

If it were not for the support of his friend Ike he wondered if he could ever manage what was ahead of him. While deep in thought a person's shadow loomed across his legs. Peter squinted into the sun, then smiled when Mister Clifton sat next to him on the ledge.

"It's a mess, isn't it, Peter?" the adult's keen blue eyes stared solemnly at the charred timber.

The teenager wrinkled a frustrated brow when he answered, "Gees, Mister Clifton, why did this happen?" He shook his head solemnly and in that instant his memory brought him back to when he was six years old and being carried down treacherous steps to escape a fire that did so much damage to the life of his family where they ended up living in that damnable tenement. Oh, how he hated that tenement. How he hated fires.

The adult cast a quick, knowing eye at Peter's question, then draped his arm around the boy's shoulders, He nodded tight-lipped when he answered, "Some things are beyond our control, Peter. There are many things that happen where they take our lives in different directions. Didn't things happen in your life that brought you to our island?

Peter nodded silently for it was so true with every student at the school. Each had their own very special tragedy that went unspoken, unrevealed. Each boy lived with his own memories, like a noiseless, yet turbulent wave filled with a silent pity. Suddenly a voice interrupted the conversation, "Hiya, Mister Clifton." Jackson had suddenly appeared and wiggled his way next to Peter. A contented smile crossed the intruders lips.

Clifton acted surprised when he reached over and rubbed the boy's head roughly. "Leo-pold!" he teased by accenting the youngsters name. The boy pulled back laughing, "Aw, Mister Clifton, nobody calls me Leopold." An unconvincing smile radiated when he continued, "They all call me Jackson, Sir." Peter nudged him gently and said, "Except me, Leopold."

The banter continued playfully when Mister Clifton asked what does Peter Pappas call him. The teenager hunched his shoulders where a shy smile appeared on his face. "Well, sir, he did call me a klutz once." he kicked the heels of his shoes against the stone wall and squirmed uncomfortably, then continued, "He never did tell me what it meant." A quick eye contact passed between the two students, but, Peter did not take the bait for an explanation for he faked looking disinterested by staring off in space.

Clifton pretended to be serious when he said, "Well, let me see if I can figure out what klutz means." He resolutely tapped his fingers to his lips as though deep in thought, then as if on a whim he chuckled when he explained, "I think it might mean a person who has klutstophobia." he smiled broadly at his definition, then looked at Jackson expectantly, questioningly waiting for a response.

Jackson erupted into fits of laughter. He rolled on his back and sputtered noisily, "Klutsophobia! I ain't never heard that word." Clifton looked at the giggling boy in false wide-eyed shock. "Oh yes you have, young man. Klutzophobia's when you don't do your homework."

Peter, silently listened to the banter, then poked his elbow into his young friend, "Now that makes you a real klutz, Leopold." he snarled impishly.

"Klutzophobia! Klutzophobia! That's a silly word?" the young boy shouted.

"I know what a klutz is." the Instructor taunted, "A klutz is what you put your foot on when you're driving a car." The two boys burst into laughter when Jackson answered wisely, "Aaaw, Mister Clifton, you really don't know what a klutz is, do you? What you said is a clutch that's in a car."

"I most certainly, absolutely do know what a klutz is, young man." The adult looked down at the snickering youth, "A klutz is a sound a chicken makes when its in the hen house." His eyebrows shot up in victory.

"That's a cluck, Mister Clifton." Jackson wrapped his hands on his elbows when he rolled on his side and broke into a fitful series of clucks.

The Instructor stood over the prostrated student and produced a demerit pad now holding a pencil to it. Looking every bit stone faced he pursed his lips, then eyed the noisy boy and said, "Now anyone here who disapproves of my definition of a klutz raise your hand so I can spell your name correctly." He winked at Peter.

"I give up! I give up!" Jackson pleaded while holding his arms over his head in surrender, "Shoot me, Mister Clifton, but, please, don't give me a demerit."

"And what's a klutz, Mister Jackson?" he peered down at the youthful scoundrel as he waited expectantly.

"Its-a, its-a clutzopho....something! Its-a, its-a klutz-clutch! Its-a Its-a klutz-cluck!" He brought his arms down from over his head and pointed to himself, "It's-me!, Mister Clifton. Its -me! Me-a klutz! But don't give me a demerit, Please, sir!"

The adult grinned down at Peter who was beside himself with laughter. "I guess Leopold knows who's the boss here." He bid a hasty goodbye and left the two boys snickering to themselves.

Peter squared his shoulders, then pulled his knees up and clasped his hands together at his shins. Pressing his chin on his knee he finally spoke to Jackson who seemed lost in thought, "Ya know, my friend Ike told me that 'klutz' was a Yiddish word that means 'clumsy'." he explained, He also said you can call a stupid person a 'klutz' too."

Peter led his young friend down the sloping lawn where they came upon a dirt road that passed by the forbidden orchard. Here they lay side by side at the edge of the lawn and followed the clouds gliding by. It was a bright sunny day where a gentle wind brought a drifting ocean breeze filled with a salty flavor that blended with with rapidly budding blossoms of the fruit trees.

It was a lazy spring day that found the Peter thinking that next year he would be graduating from what he called his island paradise. What lay ahead was a return to the detested tenement. Once again he would be caught up in the replay of that smelly tar road baking in the sun. Those screeching children playing their menacing games. Here too he remembered how he also was once a little rascal that played in the dirty alleys where garbage overflowed the rims of dented steel cans that now offered youthful grimy hands to play with the rotting remains.

He shifted uncomfortably with his thoughts when suddenly Jackson shouted "Looka!" he pointed at an odd shaped cloud formation, "Looka, Petee! Doesn't that look like a snowman? "And looka there!" his excitement grew when he pointed to yet another formation, "That one looks like a bear!" The bear was followed by what resembled a mighty warrior holding a spear which disintegrated into a dozen fluffy cannon balls.

Peter smiled at the enthusiasm of his friend when he said, "Yea, you're right, Jackson." It was his turn to point to another puffy cloud formation that seemed to be gathering smaller clouds forming what looked like a fortress. They laughed at their silliness until Peter suddenly became more serious, "You know what my Grandmother used say about clouds? She said they were blankets that covered God's bed."

Jackson quickly countered "Yea, and I bet there was some extra to give God a pillow, huh, Petee?"

"Yea know what, Jackson? My Grandmother was very religious. She taught us prayers that we had to say every night.

On religious holidays, like Easter and Christmas, we had to fast for forty days."

The young boy looked surprised, "What's fasting?" he asked.

"It meant we could not eat anything that came from an animal."

A stunned Jackson asked, "You mean like steaks and chops and chicken - stuff like that?"

"Yea, and milk and cheese and hot dogs and baloney and even ice cream and milk and all that kinda stuff too." He hesitated and finally said, "Jeez Jackson, it even got worse." his brow knitted into a frown when he continued, "Cripes, when we went to church for communion we couldn't eat anything.. At church the priest gave you a teaspoon of wine which is supposed to be the blood of Christ and then you get a piece of bread which is the body of Christ."

Peter was really getting wrapped up with his story when he continued, "And then after church we couldn't put anything in our mouths that we took out of our mouths for the rest of the day. And that meant no gum, cuz you spit it out when you finished with it. No spitting. No nothing, cuz if you did you were getting rid of Christ."

"Well, I ain't gonna join any Greek church." the youngster said emphatically.

They failed to hear footsteps approach when a shadow darkened the boy's view. "Miss Pederson!" Peter shouted when he sat up abruptly. She stood with the sun at her back forcing the boys to mask their eyes with their hand. The biologist smiled down at the two and asked, "Are you two sunbathing?" She smiled graciously when she accepted Peter's invitation to sit with them.

She wore gray slacks that day, which was offset by a flowery blouse. A broad brimmed straw hat cast a shadow over her eyes which accented her satin skin. "We've been giving names to clouds, Ma-am." the youngster volunteered. He pointed at a puffy mass which were silhouetted against the bright blue sky. "That one looks like Headmaster Williamson." Jackson snickered at his own joke.

Peter quickly defended, "Jackson's got a big imagination, ma'am." he nudged his friend to keep quiet.

The younger boy tried to cover his blunder when he answered, "Oh, it's just that the cloud looks like it's the boss." He gave the adult a quick unconvincing smile, "You know, just like Mister Williamson, the guy whose in charge."

Pederson smiled back condescendingly and then turned to Peter when she raised the question what were his thoughts on that cloud. The boy answered about it resembling the band's tuba, large, ponderous and ready to puff a deep throated blast. She glanced down at the teenager who had grown into a young adult. How quickly, she thought, do the buds bloom into such vigorous specimens now flourishing as they come into flower.

"And what do you think, Miss Pederson." Peter interrupted her thoughts. Large blue eyes gazed at her where for an instant they exchanged a confused fleeting look at one another until she hastily turned her attention back to the sky. "I think" she stammered, "I think it's like reading a book, isn't it?" She took a deep breath, then continued, "The clouds are full of mystery where you don't know where they begin or where they end. Like reading that book from the back to the front. How will you ever get to the beginning. How can you ever solve the mystery."

She gave the boys a quick, uneasy smile for she knew from the expression on their faces they did not understand what she meant. She smiled fondly at the teenagers and asked, "Didn't you boys tell me you were reading the clouds?" Peter smiled to himself thinking how she always made him see things differently and he liked it. This was why he came to her whenever a problem arose. She was his close friend and he found comfort just being with her. But then, he always had this special unexplained feeling where just being near her found a stirring in his groins forcing him to hide his embarrassment.

She had removed her hat and slowly fanned her face. A delicate fragrance laced the air and spread its essence gently with the tempo of the stirring hat. Peter closed his eyes and breathed deeply, savoring the delicate aroma which overwhelmed him.

"Falling asleep, Petee?" Miss Pederson's voice jostled his fantasy. The boy felt a rush of warm blood flush his cheeks. He quickly pointed heavenward and said, "Isn't that cloud shaped like a ship at sea?" He quickly crossed his legs, now hoping this diversion would take her attention off him. She looked up at the cloud and said, "Like that ship sailing along. It tells me I've got to get to a meeting or I'll be late." She slipped away in a rush.

The blend of her perfume lingered while Peter's mind raced daringly. His imagination now ran rampant when he lay back on the earth and closed his eyes to a fantasy that he knew was so far beyond any expectation. He shook his head slowly for he fully knew that dwelling on this dream was like reaching for the moon.

"Hey, Petee - looka there!" Jackson's voice cut knifelike into the older boy's thoughts. "Ain't that cloud lookin' like a guy with a beard?"

Peter smiled at his innocent friend and chuckled when he answered, "Oh Jackson! Will you shut up?"

From the other side of a tree a man's Scottish brogue filled the air cuttingly, "Have ye found any booty, lads? Startled, the two students looked up in surprise when an old man struck his Shillelagh at winding wildwood to clear a path. He finally found his way onto the road where he peered down at the reclining teenagers. A toothless smile was shadowed by the lip of a crumpled Tam O'Shanter hat that that sat at an angle on his head.

"Mister Derry!" Peter shouted as he hastily scrambled to his feet. He turned to the rising Jackson and said, "This is the gentleman I told you I met when I visited you in the infirmary." Smiling broadly he turned back to the disheveled old man and introduced the stunned Jackson.

The gruff old man made his way to a large boulder and sat carefully, the Shillelagh helped his from toppling over. The boys quickly found places to sit on the ground when Peter asked, "Mister Derry? You mentioned something about finding booty? What's booty, sir?"

The old man answered with a puckish grin, "Aye lad. Booty is what the or pirates called treasure." He laughed when he saw the boys mouths hang open in surprise. And then he snickered when he wiped his sweaty brow with his hat for he knew he had the two rascals really eager for more information.

"You mean there's treasure here - on the island?" Jackson asked excitedly.

"Now hold on, lad." the old man cautioned, suddenly, a puckish grin became fixed on his face. He nodded as if agreeing with some tempting thought he was about to spring on the boys, he then said, wOf the thutty islands heya in Baaston haarba, lads, we all knew one of "em was holding a buried a chest of gold."

He sat back and twisted his Shillelagh so the point created a hole in the ground. His young audience sat anxiously breathless while waiting for the rest of the story. His eyes abruptly glistened, his eyebrows shot up in anticipation. He then leaned forward to exaggerate the effect, "Lardy, lardy, lads, it had at be ol' Cap'n Blazer." Stern gray eyes circled the faces of the astounded youths. Once again he shook his head in agreement with himself. "The Cap'n was a Baaston boy, ye know. Yas sir, right out of South Baaston." He punctured the air with his Shillelagh, aiming it toward the distant city.

The shabby man pushed his straggly hair back and then continued, "Blazer waren't greedy, ya see. Ain't no way thet man wuz gonna get hisself caught. He was a smart son-of-a-bitch. He'd go out ta sea and stay close to the outta haarba," Suddenly, Derry balled his hands into fists and punched the air. His voice rose dramatically, "He'd go to the outta haarba and attack those ships out thar! Waay out thar!" He slyly smiled at the two whose full attention was focused on the story teller. "By gar, lads, ya neva know'd what he'd do next."

Peter's anticipation rose in fever pitch, when he asked, "You mean one of these islands got his treasure buried on it?" "And bury he did, lads" The rugged man with clear blue eyes flashed an intense look at the boy's who stared wide-eyed at Derry's every gripping move. The old visitor shot a narrow gaze at a distant island and then his brow wrinkled into a silent frown and suddenly the shabby, unshaven man's voice rose excitedly when he pointed his Shillelagh in the air and in a raspy voice said, "I was a wisp of a boy when my grandpap told me the story of Cap'n Blazer for he thought the old Cap'n buried his treasure on George's Island," he chuckled to himself and continued, "But ol' grandpap was wrong just as all the others in Baaston was wrong.

T'was Vound eighteen hundred ninety five, it t'was. He took a ship or two and then he'd disappear for a few yars. And then," he hesitated and chuckled again, "by golly, he'd be out thar doing it agin."

He continued his story of the pirate Captain Blazer for he knew young boys would easily fantasize at the incredible tale. In his own minds-eye it was time to leave - to let the teens dream of the possibility the treasure might be buried on their own Thompson's Island. But there was a clue the older boy, the one called Petee, might see through the ruse Suddenly, a blast from the school's tug boat signaled it was about to depart. Angus Derry scurried off toward the dock, a mischievous smile twitched his lips.

"WOW!" an amazed Jackson blurted excitedly, "Maybe we can dig around and see if the gold is here on the island.. Maybe we're rich, Petee." His eyes glistened at the thought.

"Oh, Jackson," Peter's lips slipped into a half smile, "Don't you see he suckered us? There ain't no gold." he threw up his his hands in disbelief, "It's just a story so forget about it.

CHAPTER THIRTEEN

ADIEU MY FRIENDS

1947

Seventeen year old Peter Pappas stood at the farthest point of the south end staring far down to the beach below. He was dressed in a suit, his shirt fastened by a tie and so Peter was prepared for his graduation day. He had taken what he considered his last walk around the one hundred-sixty acre island school . His thoughts drifted back in time - seven long years that seemed to have been swept away, so like the incoming ocean tide. Now, that tide recedes, swept into a new beginning.

He breathed deeply of the salty air. Air from the sea always felt so pure and clean, so unlike the air that whirls around the tenement he was going back to. A grim thought that pictured his return, going back to that wretched tenement. Didn't he leave it behind? He gave himself a short dismissing nod for his anger flashed in that moment. Kicking a stone sent it rattling over the embankment where it tumbled noisily far down to the shore. That sprite of anger diminished quickly when he rembered his purpose for being at the south end.

In moments he arrived at the white picket fence that surrounded the cemetery and stood for a moment thinking that when he left the island no one would visit his friend Ralph. There was always so much to tell him about the happenings around the school and now his words would be lost to a dying wind. Peter knelt at the graveside where somber searching eyes drew a final indelible image of the stark stone marker.

His finger etched through the engraving on the marble and here warm attentive eyes suddenly filled with tears that slipped down his cheeks now ending at some infinite void somewhere under his chin.

He took a deep breath while searching his mind for the right thing to say. He felt so guilty that he was betraying his friend, abandoning him to a time without end. He tried to speak when a sob thrust its way into this confession. He swallowed deeply to rid himself of this offensive intrusion which felt like it was fused in his throat.

"Ralph," he finally managed to say while trying hopelessly to suppress the anguish he felt. "Ralph," he stammered, "I'm....I'm graduating today." His bottom lip wavered when he balled his fist and punched the earth in despair. "I'm sorry, my friend, but...." tears welled up when his thoughts rushed like a whirlwind bringing ceaseless memories raging back. "I'm sorry Ralph," he blurted while wiping away the tears with his hand, "I've got no choice." he stood and looked down at the simple grave, "I'll never forget you."

Reaching the gate he turned for one final look, "I'll never forget you, my friend." His voice rose into a shout when he turned and raced away still shouting, "I'll never forget you, my friend." He ran with all the speed he could muster through the thickly wooded grove and reached a dirt road where the wind scattered his hair in disarray. He raced down a beaten path which finally led him behind the pristine white farm house, then sat heavily on a bench. Still struggling to catch his breath he cupped his face into his hands. Finally, he felt his nerves settling when he tossed his head back and closed his eyes, now drinking in the stillness which was quickly interrupted by songbirds flitting in the trees.

She saw him from her kitchen window, now curious that young Peter Pappas looked so troubled on this special day when he was to graduate. She could read his tear stained face from the window and then with her concern mounting stepped from the porch hoping he would open up to her as he had done so often in the past. She arrived at the bench where he was sitting and slid next to him.

Peter knew she would come to him when he looked up and spoke softly, "I've just said goodbye to my friend Ralph." The biologist placed a gentle hand on his and squeezed it with both of hers. A few moment passed where the singing birds filled the air like a blending symphony.

164

She gave him a shy, uncertain smile and asked, "You're worried no one will visit Ralph after you've gone?"

Peter unknowingly pulled his hand from hers when he turned abruptly and faced her, a questioning frown rippled his brow. He leaned forward. The corners of his mouth turned upward in surprise. "You know that?" he blurted. Large blue eyes gazed at her pleadingly. She smiled fondly at the boy and said, "I'll visit him once a week, Petee. I promise you." Peter flashed a smile . Relief was etched on his face. He was holding back tears of joy when suddenly a tell-tale tear slipped down his cheek where he quickly rubbed it away with the back of his hand and at the same time turned away in hopes she did not see it.

He was so glad she had been his friend for all these years for she was the only one who raised his sprits when he felt the world crash around him. Suddenly, she slipped away tossing a quick word, "I'll be right back, Peter." He smiled to himself when he saw the birds frantically flitting from tree branches where their harmony of tweets interrupted the thought that he was soon going to leave this island that he had called home for the past seven years. His smile faded where a frown appeared as the grim thought of going back to the detested tenement entered his mind.

But it was a brief failure when Miss Pederson returned with a neatly wrapped package that she handed him and said, "This is a little something from the woman you thought was a witch." She smiled warmly at her young friend. She too felt there would be an emptiness in her life when this young boy would no longer seek her out to solve some difficulty he was experiencing. The boy betrayed his surprise when he quickly unwrapped the gift and carefully opened the box.

"A watch!" he exclaimed in utter surprise. Blinking several times he then focused back to the watch where trembling hands cupped the precious gift. Looking up hesitatingly his eyes were suddenly fixed on her smiling face. He was at a loss for words when his mouth dropped open questioningly.

"Read the back, Petee." she encouraged.

Turning the watch he read the inscription to himself. His lips silently moving now clinging on every word. He then read it aloud.

PETER PAPPAS
(PETEE) A WONDERFUL FRIEND-LMP

He looked at her inquisitively and then asked, "LMP?" "My name's Lillian Marie Pederson." she explained. "Lillian!" he couched the name like a sacred symbol, "Lillian?" he smiled at her mischievously, "Lillian? "Can I...." he stammered, "Can I call you Lillian now?" She smiled fondly at the boy and answered, "You can now." He caught himself and thanked her for the watch and then slipped it over his wrist, now holding his hand up letting the sun's rays glisten on the metal. He then bolted to his feet and exclaimed, "My god! Look at the time. I'll be late for my graduation." She stood and while holding the excited youths hands smiled charmingly when their eyes met in an awkward fixed stare.

In an effort to change the mood she said, "Petee, you've been a great friend. I know you're going to do very well when you leave." She squeezed his hands in a final goodbye when the teenager found a courage to ask, "Miss Peder....er, Lillian." he quickly corrected,

"You once told a little boy he could kiss you when he graduates, do you remember?" She pulled back in alarm, but the boy held her hands firmly.

Large brown eyes gazed back in shock, "You remember that?" she asked in surprise.

A smile filled Peter's face when he asked, "Can that boy kiss you now on his graduation day?"

Her mind suddenly filled with the many warnings she received from the Headmaster when she first arrived. "You do not get involved with any of the boy's personal life. Each boy has had some tragic event in their lives and you are not to ask them about it. You will not get involved emotionally with these boys. And lastly, you will not.... ahem....let sex interfere with a student's life." The message was strong and extremely pointed.

"Can that boy kiss you now on his graduation day?" he repeated to the stunned botanist. She blinked several times. Her hands were still locked in his and here she was alone with a hormone-filled youth. . Finally, she said, "Petee, I did promise you that." Breathing deeply she felt a peck on the cheek would do no harm when she turned her face exposing her cheek. She closed her eyes waiting expectantly for his lips to touch her cheek. He released her hands and suddenly, gently wrapped his arms around her. He turned her chin so she faced him and now his soft lip lingered upon hers. Her emotions melted into a frenzy of mixed feelings as she felt limp. Her desires were swept into a passion she abruptly knew had to be controlled.

But Peter was swept away into a sensuous obsession for the overwhelming fragrance of her perfume was not only overpowering, the tenderness of her lips captured his very soul. His emotions instantly scaled with the strength of his heartbeat when he pressed his lips more firmly on hers. Suddenly, as if a warning signal roared in her head, she pulled away and looked at the boy in amazement. "You've done this before?" she questioned nervously.

Peter knew he only had minutes to race back to the dormitory to get himself ready for graduation. Yet, his yearning to kiss Lillian again raced through his very being. But no, he reasoned, despite his frustration he had to be satisfied with that one moment of pleasure. It was time to go. It was time to leave his island home and the one woman he came to adore.

The youth stood awkwardly between a stone walkway that led through the trees. He looked upon Lillian who was sitting on a bench watching him. She smiled at his innocence then waved at the lonely figure silhouetted by the trees and said, "Goodbye, Peter Pappas. Goodbye, my dear friend."

Peter stuffed his hands into his pockets and started to walk away when suddenly, from somewhere high in the trees a crow's cutting caw split the air.. The boy looked back at his enchanting friend and yelled above the obnoxious cries of the crow, "I love you, Lillian." He felt his face glow with embarrassment when he raced down the road without looking back.

From high in the blue sky the large crow soared on unseen air currents while cawing obnoxiously from far above. Peter stopped running and took another long look at the distant farm house. He turned to the circling crow and shouted, "You were laughing at me, weren't you! Damn You!" he cursed. "She didn't hear me because of you!" He picked up a loose stone and threw it ineffectually at the loathsome bird. He then turned and raced toward the main campus.

THE END